The Believer's Life in Christ

The Believer's Life in Christ

by
John MacArthur, Jr.

MOODY PRESS
CHICAGO

© 1989 by
JOHN F. MACARTHUR, JR.

All Scripture quotations, unless noted otherwise, are from the *New Scofield Reference Bible*, King James Version. Copyright © 1967 by Oxford University Press, Inc. Reprinted by permission.

ISBN: 0-8024-5382-1

1 2 3 4 5 6 7 8 Printing/LC/Year 94 93 92 91 90 89

Printed in the United States of America

Contents

These Bible studies are taken from messages delivered by Pastor-Teacher John MacArthur, Jr., at Grace Community Church in Panorama City, California. The recorded messages themselves may be purchased as a series or individually. Please request the current price list by writing to:

WORD OF GRACE COMMUNICATIONS
P.O. Box 4000
Panorama City, CA 91412

Or call the following toll-free number:
1-800-55-GRACE

1
The Mystery of the Church

Outline

Introduction
A. A Book About Riches
   1. The understanding of our riches
   2. The magnitude of our riches
   3. The fullness of our riches
   4. The guarantee of our riches
   5. The basis of our riches
B. A Book About the Church
   1. The mystery of the church
   2. The mysteries of the kingdom
     a) The promised millennial kingdom
       (1) The kingdom anticipated
       (2) The kingdom offered
       (3) The kingdom rejected
       (4) The kingdom postponed
     b) The present mystery kingdom
       (1) Concealed from the Old Testament saints
       (2) Compared to the millennial kingdom
       (3) Contrasted with other mysteries
   3. The metaphor of the church
     a) The definition
     b) The synonyms
     c) The distinction

Lesson
I. A Dual Source of Authority (v. 1*a*)
A. Paul's Chronicles
   1. Before conversion
   2. After conversion

B. Paul's Credentials
  1. His apostleship
  2. His attitude
  3. His authenticity
    a) A unique calling
    b) A unique relationship to Christ
    c) A unique power
  4. His approach
C. Paul's Commission
II. A Dual Designation for Believers (v. 1*b*)
III. A Dual Blessing for Believers (v. 2*a*)
IV. A Dual Source of Blessing (v. 2*b*)

Introduction

Hetty Green was known as America's greatest miser. She managed an inherited fortune so shrewdly that she was also considered the greatest woman financier in the world. In 1916 she died, leaving an estate that was worth nearly 100 million dollars. Yet she would eat cold oatmeal because she didn't want to spend the money to heat the water. Her son eventually lost his leg from a relatively minor injury because she took him to a number of free medical clinics instead of calling for a doctor. (Her life is recounted in *Hetty Green: A Woman Who Loved Money*, by Boyden Sparkes [New York: Doubleday, 1930].) Hetty Green had tremendous resources but didn't make use of them.

A. A Book About Riches

  1. The understanding of our riches

    The book of Ephesians is about the riches, fullness, and inheritance that a believer has in Christ. Because of that, some have called Ephesians the treasure house of the Bible. During the Great Depression some banks restricted the amount of money their clients could withdraw from their own accounts. God, however, doesn't work that way. His resources are boundless and always available to His children. The book of Ephesians will teach you who you are, how rich you are, and how you should use those riches for Christ's glory.

8

2. The magnitude of our riches

In the epistle of Ephesians the apostle Paul speaks of "the riches of his [God's] grace" (1:7), "the unsearchable riches of Christ" (3:8), and "the riches of his glory" (3:16). We will see how God showers His riches on His children.

Paul also used several terms in Ephesians to describe our abundant resources. He referred to "riches" five times, "grace" twelve times, "glory" eight times, "inheritance" four times, "fullness," "filled up," or "fills" six times, and "in Christ" fifteen times.

3. The fullness of our riches

In Christ we have the fullness of "the riches of the glory of his inheritance" (1:18). Paul prayed that we "might be filled with all the fullness of God" (3:19). He also desired that all believers know "the unsearchable riches of Christ, . . . who is able to do exceedingly abundantly above all that we ask or think, according to the power that worketh in us" (3:8, 20). God has the resources to cover all our past debts, present liabilities, and future needs. In fact, God has made available to us the fullness of Himself (3:19), Christ (4:13), and the Holy Spirit (5:18).

4. The guarantee of our riches

The guarantee of our riches is founded upon the fact that they are "in Christ," a phrase repeated fifteen times in Ephesians. Our riches are secure because Christ is secure in the plan and love of the Father. Our resources are secure because God has made them available to Christ. What God has given to His Son is also ours because we have become "joint heirs with Christ" (Rom. 8:17). Referring to all believers, Hebrews 2:11 says, "He is not ashamed to call them brethren." First Corinthians 6:17 says, "He that is joined unto the Lord is one spirit." His possessions are ours. All His riches are at our disposal. The apostle Peter called this "an inheritance incorruptible, and undefiled, and that fadeth not away, reserved in heaven for you" (1 Pet. 1:4).

5. The basis of our riches

We did not earn the riches we have in Christ. Rather, they are ours because of God's mercy, which is emphasized throughout Ephesians. We are rich because of God's will (1:5, 9, 11), grace (1:6-7), glory (1:12, 14), power (1:19), love (2:4), good pleasure (1:9), purpose (1:11; 3:11), calling (1:18), inheritance (1:18), and workmanship (2:10).

B. A Book About the Church

Because believers are in Christ, they are in His Body, the church. Ephesians focuses on the basic doctrine of the church—what it is and how believers function within it.

1. The mystery of the church

In Ephesians 3:3 Paul expresses a key thought relative to the church: "By revelation he [God] made known to me the mystery." That mystery "in other ages was not made known unto the sons of men, as it is now revealed unto his holy apostles and prophets by the Spirit" (v. 5). Verse 6 identifies the mystery: "That the Gentiles should be fellow heirs, and of the same body, and partakers of his promise in Christ by the gospel." A mystery in the biblical sense is something that had been hidden in the past but is now revealed in the New Testament. The book of Ephesians presents the mystery of the church. The hidden secret of the past (v. 5), revealed to Paul in the present (v. 3), was that Jew and Gentile alike would be one in Christ's Body—the church.

God's Pattern of Revelation

1. God has secrets He will never reveal

Deuteronomy 29:29 says, "The secret things belong unto the Lord our God; but those things which are revealed belong unto us and to our children forever." God chooses to reveal some things to man, but others remain a mystery.

2. God has secrets He reveals only to believers

Psalm 25:14 says, "The secret of the Lord is with those who fear him, and he will show them his covenant." God reveals His secrets to believers. Proverbs 3:32 says that God's "secret is with the righteous." Amos 3:7 says, "He revealeth his secret unto his servants." God has revealed some things to all people. Romans 1:20 says everyone knows something about God's "eternal power and Godhead, so that they are without excuse." But there are certain things God reserves only for His children to know. For example, the disciples understood things no one else understood because the Father had "hidden these things from the wise and prudent, and . . . revealed them unto babes" (Matt. 11:25).

3. God has secrets He revealed only in the New Testament

The New Testament is new truth for a new age—sacred secrets revealed by God. The Old Testament saints searched their own writings in an attempt to discover their meaning (1 Pet. 1:10-11). Even the angels long to understand the truths we know, including the meaning of salvation (Eph. 3:9-10; 1 Pet. 1:12). The man given the responsibility of revealing most of the mysteries was the apostle Paul.

2. The mysteries of the kingdom

God always has kept secrets that He would reveal only to His people. Paul said, "The natural man receiveth not the things of the Spirit of God; for they are foolishness unto him, neither can he know them, because they are spiritually discerned" (1 Cor. 2:14). Indeed, Jesus often spoke in a manner that unbelievers could not understand. That led the disciples to ask, "Why speakest thou unto them [unbelievers] in parables?" (Matt. 13:10). Jesus replied, "Because it is given unto you to know the mysteries of the kingdom of heaven, but to them it is not given" (v. 11). Verses 34-35 say, "All these things spoke Jesus unto the multitude in parables, and without a parable spoke he not unto them, that it might be fulfilled which was spoken by the prophet, saying, I will open my mouth in parables; I will utter things which have been kept secret from the foundation of the

11

world." The mysteries of the kingdom of God were not fully revealed until the New Testament era. So although the Old Testament saints had sufficient knowledge of God, their understanding was not as complete as it would be for those who lived after the coming of Christ.

In Matthew 13:11 Christ mentions the "mysteries of the kingdom of heaven." I believe it was not the kingdom itself but the form of the kingdom that was a mystery.

a) The promised millennial kingdom

(1) The kingdom anticipated

That God would establish an earthly kingdom was no mystery in the Old Testament. It was frequently prophesied that the Messiah would come and set up His kingdom (Gen. 49:10; Ps. 2:6-9; Isa. 9:6-7; 11:10; Jer. 23:5-6; Dan. 7:13-14, 18).

(2) The kingdom offered

John the Baptist said, "Repent; for the kingdom of heaven is at hand" (Matt. 3:2). Likewise Christ proclaimed the same thing (Matt. 4:17). Jesus offered the kingdom of God to Israel. He was born a king, acknowledged as a king by the wise men, and confronted with His claim to be a king by Pilate.

(3) The kingdom rejected

So it was not a mystery that a king was coming to set up an earthly reign. What was not realized was that the kingdom would be rejected. The Jewish leaders said about Christ, "We will not have this man to reign over us" (Luke 19:14; cf. John 1:10-11).

(4) The kingdom postponed

The earthly kingdom was postponed because Israel rejected their king. However, it will be established at a future time. The book of Revelation tells us about the one-thousand year reign of Christ upon the earth (19:1–20:6). Jesus must be crowned as king of a literal, earthly kingdom to fulfill His right to rule. So God's promise of a kingdom to Israel will be fulfilled, although it is presently postponed because Israel rejected her king.

b) The present mystery kingdom

(1) Concealed from the Old Testament saints

The Old Testament did not make clear that the king would have to come twice and that there would be a lengthy gap between His arrivals. Therefore, the present age is called a mystery. A particular feature of the present age, unknown in the Old Testament, is that Jew and Gentile are united into one Body. Israel didn't realize that as a consequence of her disobedience, God would temporarily set her aside and call a new people by His name. So all the details of the church age were a mystery prior to the New Testament.

(2) Compared to the millennial kingdom

In what sense is Christ reigning today? Although He is in heaven and the physical kingdom is yet to come, Colossians says that at salvation God "delivered us from the power of darkness, and hath translated us into the kingdom of his dear Son" (1:13). Yet Ephesians says that Satan is "the prince of the power of the air" (2:2). The apparent contradiction is eliminated when we realize that Christ's future kingdom will be physical. But during the church age Christ's reign is primarily spiritual—Christ reigns in the hearts of His people.

Although the millennial kingdom will have an external focus, the present kingdom has an internal focus. Just as Christ will be outwardly enthroned in Jerusalem during the Millennium (Ps. 2:6-9), He now is inwardly enthroned in the hearts of His saints (Rom. 10:9-10). As He then will bring external peace to the whole world (Isa. 2:4; 32:17; Mic. 4:3), He now brings internal peace in the lives of believers (John 14:27; 16:33; Phil. 4:7). As in the future kingdom He will dispense grace (Isa. 19:21-25; 52:10; Jer. 23:6), so He does even now to those who trust in Him (Acts 4:12; Rom. 10:10, 13; 2 Thess. 2:13). As He will then bestow joy and happiness externally (Isa. 35:1-2, 6-7), He now internally bestows those blessings on His own people (Rom. 15:13; Gal. 5:22; Eph. 1:3).

The kingdom of which the Old Testament speaks, and which will be fully manifested in the Millennium, now exists in a partial state. As Peter explained in his sermon on the Day of Pentecost, the remarkable events that had just occurred in Jerusalem (Acts 2:1-13) were a preview of what Joel prophesied about the millennial kingdom: "It shall come to pass in the last days, saith God, I will pour out of my Spirit upon all flesh" (vv. 16-17; cf. Joel 2:28-32).

(3) Contrasted with other mysteries

Within the mystery kingdom are many other revealed mysteries (Matt. 13:11): the indwelling Christ (Col. 1:26-27), the incarnation of the Son of God (Col. 2:2-3; 1 Tim. 3:16), Israel's unbelief and rejection of the Messiah (Rom. 11:25), iniquity (2 Thess. 2:7), Babylon—the terrible, vile, economic and religious system of the end times (Rev. 17), the unity of believers (Eph. 3:3-6), the church as Christ's bride (Eph. 5:24-32), and the rapture (1 Cor. 15:51-52). The mystery age will be completed when Christ returns in glory (Rev. 10:7).

3. The metaphor of the church

Ephesians uses the metaphor of the human body to present the church.

a) The definition

A metaphor defines something by using another object with similar characteristics. The church is like a body because both are organisms with interlinking systems. As members of the Body of Christ, the life of God flows through us. We are inextricably united. If one believer in the Body doesn't do what he's supposed to do, the Body is affected. And when the Body of Christ malfunctions, that gives the world cause to see Christ as a cripple. The Body must be healthy and complete so that we come to "the stature of the fullness of Christ" (Eph. 4:13). The church as Christ's Body must function as well as Christ in His incarnation. In a sense the church is "Body II"— "Body I" being the incarnate Christ.

b) The synonyms

Scripture uses other metaphors to describe the church. All metaphors used in the New Testament are used in the Old Testament, except for the body.

(1) Bride

    (*a*) Used of Israel in Hosea 1:1–3:5

    (*b*) Used of the church in Ephesians 5:22-33

(2) Vine

    (*a*) Used of Israel in Isaiah 5:1-7

    (*b*) Used of the church in John 15:1-8

(3) Flock

    (*a*) Used of Israel in Isaiah 40:11

    (*b*) Used of the church in John 10:1-16

(4) Kingdom

    (*a*) Used of Israel in Exodus 19:6

    (*b*) Used of the church in Colossians 1:13

(5) Family

    (*a*) Used of Israel in Hosea 1:10

    (*b*) Used of the church in Ephesians 2:19

(6) Building

    (*a*) Used of Israel in Ezekiel 9:9; 43:10

    (*b*) Used of the church in Ephesians 2:20-22 and
       1 Peter 2:5

c) The distinction

The metaphors of Israel and the church are synonymous except for the metaphor of the body. The body concept is a unique truth reserved for the church age. We are a Body through which Christ can manifest Himself to the world. That's why it's so important that we are all functioning properly within the Body by using the spiritual gifts He has given us (Rom. 12:3-8; 1 Cor. 12:4-11; Eph. 4:11-13). Only when we do so does Christ come to full stature in His church (Eph. 4:13).

The key to all the metaphors of the church is unity. We are one wife with one Husband, one flock with one Shepherd, one set of branches with one Vine, one kingdom with one King, one family with one Father, one building with one Foundation, and one body with one Head. But the Body is the most perfect illustration of how the church is to function, for it speaks of both diversity and mutual dependence.

Lesson

I. A DUAL SOURCE OF AUTHORITY (v. 1*a*)

"Paul, an apostle of Jesus Christ by the will of God."

A. Paul's Chronicles

1. Before conversion

   Paul was from the tribe of Benjamin (Phil. 3:5) and possibly named after the most prominent member of that tribe, Saul. He became a rabbi and sat at the feet of the great teacher Gamaliel (Acts 22:3). In addition, some believe that Paul was a member of the Sanhedrin. In any case, he was one of the most devout anti-Christian leaders in Judaism (Acts 22:4-5). He passionately hated Christians and was on his way to arrest some of them in Damascus when the Lord stopped him suddenly, transforming him into a messenger of the gospel (Acts 9:1-15).

2. After conversion

   Paul spent three years in Arabia and Damascus (Gal. 1:17-18), and then with Barnabas, Symeon, Lucius, and Manaen ministered in the church at Antioch (Acts 13:1). At Antioch the Lord said to the leaders of the church: "Separate me Barnabas and Saul for the work unto which I have called them. And when they had fasted and prayed, and laid their hands on them, they sent them away" (Acts 13:2-3). That was the beginning of Paul's first missionary journey to the Gentiles.

Was Ephesians Written Only to the Church in Ephesus?

The best manuscripts of this letter do not contain the words "at Ephesus" (1:1). Some manuscripts leave a blank space instead.

There is also no mention of anything local to Ephesus, such as references to individual people or local congregations. Most scholars believe the letter was meant to be circulated among all the churches of Asia Minor. That being the case, each church was to insert its own name in the blank space. Some also believe that Paul's letter to the Laodiceans (Col. 4:16) may have been the book of Ephesians, which would have gone to nearby Smyrna, Pergamos, Thyatira, Sardis, and Ephesus (cf. Rev. 2-3). The universal content of the letter suggests that it may have gone first to Ephesus and then to those other churches.

B. Paul's Credentials

1. His apostleship

Paul referred to himself as an apostle with a message from God (1:1). He was one of fourteen men who occupied the office of apostle. In the beginning Christ had twelve. Matthias became the thirteenth when he was added after Judas defected (Acts 1:15-26). Paul was the fourteenth.

The apostles were foundational to the church (2:20). Some of them, including Paul, were used by God to record Scripture (John 14:26; Acts 2:42; 2 Pet. 3:15-16). But once the church was established and the canon of Scripture was closed, there was no longer a need for the office of apostle.

Paul's credentials were simply that he was "an apostle of Jesus Christ by the will of God." That alone gave him the authority to command believers' attention.

2. His attitude

It was not vanity that caused Paul to call himself an apostle, for in 1 Corinthians 15:10 he says, "But by the grace of God I am what I am." In his first epistle to Timothy he writes, "I thank Christ Jesus, our Lord, who hath enabled me, in that he counted me faithful, putting me into the ministry, who was before a blasphemer, and a persecutor. . . . Christ Jesus came into the world to save sinners, of whom I am chief" (1:12-13, 15).

18

3. His authenticity

    a) A unique calling—Paul was commissioned by God to take the gospel to the Gentiles (Acts 9:15).

    b) A unique relationship to Christ—God transformed Paul into a bond slave of Christ. Paul no longer lived for himself. He said, "For me to live is Christ, and to die is gain" (Phil. 1:21).

    c) A unique power—As an apostle, Paul ministered in the power of Jesus Christ (Acts 13:11; 14:3; 19:11-12).

4. His approach

With the exception of Philippians, 1 and 2 Thessalonians, and Philemon, Paul began his epistles with an acknowledgment of his apostleship. One reason he did that was to defend his authority against those who degraded him because he wasn't one of the twelve original apostles. Yet Paul clearly met the requirements of an apostle, saying, "Am I not an apostle? . . . Have I not seen Jesus Christ, our Lord? Are not ye my work in the Lord?" (1 Cor. 9:1).

C. Paul's Commission

The apostles carried out specific functions.

1. They preached the gospel (1 Cor. 1:17).

2. They taught and prayed (Acts 6:4).

3. They performed miracles (2 Cor. 12:12).

4. They built leaders for the church (Acts 14:23).

5. They recorded God's Word (Eph. 1:1).

II. A DUAL DESIGNATION FOR BELIEVERS (v. 1*b*)

"To the saints who are at Ephesus, and to the faithful in Christ Jesus."

Believers are called "saints" and "the faithful" to emphasize the divine and human aspects of their lives. From the divine side, God made them to be holy. From the human side, man is responsible to exercise faith. Every Christian has been made holy by God, so all Christians are saints. Likewise every Christian's life should be characterized by faithfulness.

III. A DUAL BLESSING FOR BELIEVERS (v. 2a)

"Grace be to you, and peace."

The greeting Paul used was common among first-century believers. The term *grace* (Gk., *charis*) refers to unmerited favor. It is God's graciousness that leads Him to extend kindness to undeserving people. As a greeting, then, *charis* has rich theological significance in contrast to our use of "hello," which merely communicates a greeting or surprise.

"Peace" (Gk., *eirēnē*) is the inevitable result of God's grace. We have peace because God has shown us His grace. Grace is the source of blessing, whereas peace is the continued state of one who has been given grace by God.

IV. A DUAL SOURCE OF BLESSING (v. 2b)

"From God, our father, and from the Lord Jesus Christ."

The source of our abundant riches is God and Christ. Paul's desire was that Christians understand God's grace and possess His peace. The book of Ephesians is the product of that desire.

Focusing on the Facts

1. Why do people refer to Ephesians as the believers' bank (see p. 8)?
2. What are three verses in Ephesians that emphasize God's riches (see p. 9)?
3. List the various terms that are used to describe our abundant riches (see p. 9).

4. Explain why we have assurance that our spiritual riches are secure (see p. 9).
5. Explain why the church is referred to as a mystery (see p. 10).
6. What is a mystery in the biblical sense (see p. 10)?
7. Describe God's pattern of revelation (see pp. 10-11).
8. Why did Christ speak in parables (Matt. 13:10-11, 34-35; see pp. 11-12)?
9. What does the Old Testament prophesy about the kingdom of God (see p. 12)?
10. The original offer of the kingdom was given to whom (Matt. 4:17; see p. 12)?
11. Why was the Messiah's earthly kingdom postponed (see p. 12)?
12. In what sense can we say that Christ is reigning today (see p. 13)?
13. How does Christ's present reign differ from His reign during the Millennium (see pp. 13-14)?
14. What is the definition of a metaphor (see p. 15)?
15. What are the seven primary metaphors used to describe the church (see pp. 15-16)?
16. What is the one metaphor used for the church in the New Testament that is not found in the Old Testament (see p. 16)?
17. The book of Ephesians was written to whom? Explain (see pp. 17-18).
18. Why did Paul frequently begin his epistles by stating that he was an apostle (see p. 19)?
19. Name five duties carried out by Paul and the other apostles (see p. 19).
20. What is the distinctive emphasis of the terms "saints" and "the faithful" (Eph. 1:1; see p. 20)?

Pondering the Principles

1. Look up the definition of malnutrition in a dictionary. Given the definition, how would you define spiritual malnutrition? Ask some mature Christian friends how they prevent spiritual malnutrition in their walk with God. Then spend time in prayer asking God to show you areas of weakness in your own life. Once you identify those areas, establish specific measures to correct them.

2. Why is the metaphor of the body so appropriate for the church? How is your own physical body affected when one of its parts doesn't function? How is the Body of Christ affected when individual believers aren't functioning? Read Romans 12:3-8 and 1 Corinthians 12:1-31. Determine what your spiritual gifts are by examining what you and others think you do best. Are you exercising your gifts to build up the Body of Christ? If not, consider that your lack of participation is affecting the ministry of the Body in the world, and make plans to change your situation immediately.

2

The Body Formed in Eternity Past—Part 1

Outline

Introduction
A. The Church—Uniquely Described
B. The Church—Uniquely Delineated
   1. Ephesians 1:22-23
   2. Ephesians 2:15-16
   3. Ephesians 3:6
   4. Ephesians 4:16
   5. Ephesians 5:30
C. The Church—Uniquely Designed

Lesson
I. The Elements of the Blessing (v. 3)
  A. The Blessed One—God
  B. The Blesser—God
  C. The Blessed Ones—Believers
  D. The Blessings—Everything Spiritual
    1. Our unnecessary requests
     a) Love
     b) Peace
     c) Joy
     d) Strength
    2. Our unlimited resources
  E. The Location of Blessing—The Heavenly Places
    1. The place of our citizenship
    2. The pull of our citizenship
    3. The perspective of our citizenship
    4. The practicality of our citizenship
  F. The Agent of Blessing—Christ

II. The Eternal Formation of the Body (vv. 4-14)
   A. In the Past—Election (vv. 4-6a)
      1. The method: sovereign selection (v. 4a)
         a) Its concept
            (1) The paradox
            (2) The purpose
            (3) The period
               (a) Revelation 13:8
               (b) Revelation 17:8
            (4) The participants
               (a) Israel
               (b) Angels
               (c) Jesus Christ
               (d) The apostles
               (e) The church
            (5) The plan
               (a) 2 Timothy 1:9
               (b) 2 Timothy 2:10
               (c) 2 Thessalonians 2:13
               (d) Acts 13:48

   Conclusion

Introduction

A. The Church—Uniquely Described

One of the keys to understanding the book of Ephesians is to realize that this epistle is built on the concept of the church as the Body of Christ (see pp. 14-16). As a human body functions in an incredible, multiple-phase operation—totally dependent upon every muscle, tissue, and nerve—the church is similarly complex. As the human body receives all its direction from the head, so the church receives direction from Jesus Christ. As the body manifests a person's soul to the world, so the church manifests Christ to the world.

B. The Church—Uniquely Delineated

1. Ephesians 1:22-23—God "hath put all things under his [Christ's] feet, and gave him to be the head over all things to the church, which is his body."

2. Ephesians 2:15-16—Christ "abolished in his flesh the enmity, even the law of commandments contained in ordinances, to make in himself of two one new man, so making peace; and that he might reconcile both unto God in one body."

3. Ephesians 3:6—The mystery of the church is "that the Gentiles should be fellow heirs, and of the same body, and partakers of his promise in Christ by the gospel."

4. Ephesians 4:16—From Christ "the whole body fitly joined together and compacted by that which every joint supplieth, according to the effectual working in the measure of every part, maketh increase of the body unto the edifying of itself in love."

5. Ephesians 5:30—"We are members of his body, of his flesh, and of his bones."

The head of the church, Christ, manifests His will through the Body of Christ. The church is not an organization that functions by structure alone. Rather, it is an organism that depends on the flow of life passing between its members.

C. The Church—Uniquely Designed

Paul normally discussed the church from the vantage point of its present state and operation. However, he began Ephesians by unveiling the divine plan for the church, which preceded the creation of the universe. Verses 3-14 say, "Blessed be the God and Father of our Lord Jesus Christ, who hath blessed us with all spiritual blessings in heavenly places in Christ, according as he hath chosen us in him before the foundation of the world, that we should be holy and without blame before him, in love having predestinated us unto the adoption of sons by Jesus Christ to himself, according to the good pleasure of his will, to the praise of the glory of his grace, through which he hath made us accepted in the Beloved; in whom we have redemption through his blood, the forgiveness of sins, according to the riches of his grace, in which he hath abounded toward us in all wisdom and prudence, having made known unto us the mystery of his will, according to his good pleasure which he hath purposed in himself; that in the dispensation of the fullness of times he might gather together in one all things in Christ, both which are in heaven, and which are on earth, even in him; in whom also we have obtained an inheritance, being predestinated according to the purpose of him who worketh all things after the counsel of his own will, that we should be to the praise of his glory, who first trusted in Christ; in whom ye also trusted, after ye heard the word of truth, the gospel of your salvation; in whom also after ye believed, ye were sealed with that Holy Spirit of promise, who is the earnest of our inheritance until the redemption of the purchased possession, unto the praise of his glory."

Note that all that is packed in one sentence. Led by the Spirit, Paul lingered on the marvels of God's grace. That glorious passage takes us back to eternity and discusses God's eternal formation of the church. The church is not an afterthought of God. Rather, before history began, God established the church.

The Nagging Issue of Self-Worth

Many are asking themselves, *Am I valuable? Can I find a way to accept myself as I am?* There is a plethora of opinion as to the right answers to those questions. Some propagate self-image books and seminars that tell people they are basically good. Others believe that man's identity is bound up in an understanding of his heritage, so tracing one's family tree is said to be therapeutic. Such opinions, however, are too simplistic. They fail to take man's nature into consideration.

This problem is multiplied by Christian books addressing the themes of psychology, self-image, and self-worth in a nonbiblical manner. They present techniques to help people rid themselves of guilt, fear, timidity, and inadequacy. But no one will develop a true sense of self-worth by playing psychological games. Some have realized that is true, so they teach that self-worth comes only from doing good deeds. They seek their value by trying to establish their own righteousness. That's their way of trying to gain acceptance with God and man. Such an emphasis is not unlike that of the Pharisees, who extolled external acts while ignoring internal problems (cf. Matt. 23). Although they establish a feeling of self-worth, the inner man is destroyed. Guilt, fear, anxiety, and depression are submerged because they must continue to hide from the truth about themselves.

A true sense of self-worth comes from understanding our position in Christ. We have been chosen in Christ from before the foundation of the world. Knowing that gives us a sense of our significance and value to God. We were so important to God that He gave up His Son to die on our behalf.

God's redemptive history is His reaching down and drawing to Himself those whom He chose to save. In Ephesians 1:3-14 Paul gives us a glimpse of that plan of salvation. In verse 3 Paul begins with a benediction, praising God for all Christ has done for us. Then in verses 4-14 he discusses the aspects of God's eternal purpose for the church: the past—election (vv. 3-6a), the present—redemption (vv. 6b-11), and the future—inheritance (vv. 12-14).

This passage can also be divided into three sections, each of which focuses on a different Person of the Trinity. Verses 3-6a center on the Father, verses 6b-12 center on the Son, and verses 13-14 center on the Holy Spirit. Paul takes us to heaven's very throne to show the greatness and the vastness of the blessings and treasures that belong to those who are in Christ Jesus.

Lesson

I. THE ELEMENTS OF THE BLESSING (v. 3)

"Blessed be the God and father of our Lord Jesus Christ, who hath blessed us with all spiritual blessings in heavenly places in Christ."

A. The Blessed One—God

The Greek word translated "blessed" is *eulogētos*, from which we derive the English word *eulogy*. It means to "speak well of someone." Paul begins verse 3 by saying that God is good. In fact, Jesus says in Matthew 19 that "there is none good but one, that is God" (v. 17). And God is good whether we perceive Him to be or not.

The Bible records the goodness of God from beginning to end. In Genesis Melchizedek says, "Blessed be the Most High God" (14:20). In Revelation we read, "Blessing, and honor, and glory, and power be unto him that sitteth upon the throne, and unto the Lamb forever and ever" (5:13). Whatever trial or trouble we may be facing, we are to continually bless the Lord.

B. The Blesser—God

Ephesians 1:3 says that God "hath blessed." James says that "every good gift and every perfect gift is from above, and cometh down from the father of lights, with whom is no variableness, neither shadow of turning" (1:17). Romans 8:28 says, "We know that all things work together for good to them that love God, to them who are the called according to his purpose." God is the source of every good thing. Genesis 1:31 tells us that after the creation, "God saw every thing that he had made, and, behold, it was very good."

C. The Blessed Ones—Believers

Ephesians 1:3 says that God "hath blessed *us*" (emphasis added). Galatians 3:9 tells us who has been blessed: "They who are of faith are blessed." Those who have been chosen by God are blessed. When we bless God, we speak well of Him. When He blesses us, He does good to us. Our blessing is our praise to Him. His blessing is His deeds to us.

D. The Blessings—Everything Spiritual

Paul then said that we have been blessed "with all spiritual blessings." The Greek word translated "spiritual" (*pneuma-*

tikos) in the New Testament always refers to the work of the Holy Spirit. All God's blessings are dispensed to us through the agency of the Holy Spirit.

1. Our unnecessary requests

    In Romans 8:26 Paul writes, "We know not what we should pray for as we ought." We constantly ask God for things He has already given us. We are ignorant of our resources.

    a) Love—"The love of God is shed abroad in our hearts" (Rom. 5:5).

    b) Peace—Christ said to the disciples, "Peace I leave with you, my peace I give unto you; not as the world giveth, give I unto you. Let not your heart be troubled, neither let it be afraid" (John 14:27).

    c) Joy—The Lord said, "These things have I spoken unto you, that my joy might remain in you, and that your joy might be full" (John 15:11).

    d) Strength—Paul proclaimed, "I can do all things through Christ, who strengtheneth me" (Phil. 4:13).

    God has given us all spiritual blessings, yet we need to ask for wisdom in understanding how to use those resources (James 1:5).

2. Our unlimited resources

    We receive all spiritual blessings when we accepted Christ as our Savior. Second Peter says that "His divine power hath given unto us all things that pertain unto life and godliness" (1:3). There are no missing ingredients.

    In Philippians 1:19 Paul refers to "the supply of the Spirit." Every available spiritual blessing was dispensed to us by the Spirit. The issue for the believer is to use what he has, not to wait for some second work of grace.

E. The Location of Blessing—The Heavenly Places

1. The place of our citizenship

"In heavenly places" (v. 3) encompasses the entire supernatural realm of God, His complete domain, the full extent of His divine operation. While it includes heaven, it's not limited to that. Ephesians 6:12 says, "We wrestle not against flesh and blood, but against . . . spiritual wickedness in high places [lit., "the heavenlies"]."

Nevertheless, Christians are not so much citizens of the earth as they are citizens of heaven. Philippians 3:20 says plainly, "Our citizenship is in heaven, from which also we look for the Savior, the Lord Jesus Christ." Because we are citizens of heaven, we are able to understand spiritual matters. First Corinthians 2:14 tells us that "the natural man receiveth not the things of the Spirit of God . . . because they are spiritually discerned." Rather, unbelievers are "children of this world" (Luke 16:8, KJV*). From Colossians we learn that believers have been "translated . . . into the kingdom of [God's] dear Son" (1:13). Colossians 3:1-2 says, "Seek those things which are above. . . . Set your affection on things above, not on things on the earth."

No matter where I travel, I am an American citizen. Whether I am in North America, Latin America, Europe, Asia, or Africa, I remain an American citizen with all the corresponding rights and privileges. Similarly, we as believers are citizens of heaven even though we live in a foreign land.

2. The pull of our citizenship

Our Father, home, Savior, friends, and loved ones are in heaven. There is so much that we long for in heaven, yet we must continue our sojourn on earth. We're trapped in a tension between the earthly and the heavenly realms (Phil. 1:20-23).

*King James Version.

3. The perspective of our citizenship

In 2 Corinthians 6 we see Paul's perspective on his heavenly citizenship. He saw himself "as sorrowful, yet always rejoicing; as poor, yet making many rich; as having nothing, and yet possessing all things" (v. 10). Earlier Paul said, "We are troubled on every side, yet not distressed; we are perplexed, but not in despair; persecuted, but not forsaken; cast down, but not destroyed" (4:8-9). There is an inherent tension of being in two worlds. We may have nothing in this world, but in the heavenlies we're rich beyond description.

4. The practicality of our citizenship

In Galatians 5 Paul says, "The fruit of the Spirit is love, joy, peace, long-suffering, gentleness, goodness, faith, meekness, self-control" (vv. 22-23). All our spiritual riches can be appropriated by walking in the power of the Holy Spirit.

F. The Agent of Blessing—Christ

When we became Christians we were placed into a marvelous union with Christ. First Corinthians 6:17 says, "The one who joins himself to the Lord is one spirit with Him" (NASB*). Romans 8:16-17 says, "We are the children of God; and if children, then heirs—heirs of God, and joint heirs with Christ." When we came to know Jesus Christ we became joint heirs with Him, and God dispensed to us all the riches that the Spirit could transmit. Because we are one with Jesus Christ, His righteousness is imputed to us and His inheritance is ours.

Because we are in Christ, His position is our position, His privilege is our privilege, His possessions are our possessions, and His practice is our practice. We are significant not because of who we are but because of who we are in Christ. As Paul said, "By the grace of God I am what I am" (1 Cor. 15:10).

*New American Standard Bible.

31

II. THE ETERNAL FORMATION OF THE BODY (vv. 4-14)

A. In the Past—Election (vv. 4-6a)

"According as he hath chosen us in him before the foundation of the world, that we should be holy and without blame before him, in love having predestinated us unto the adoption of sons by Jesus Christ to himself, according to the good pleasure of his will, to the praise of the glory of his grace."

1. The method: sovereign selection (v. 4a)

"According as he hath chosen us in him before the foundation of the world."

In verse 3 Paul praises God because he was so overwhelmed that God had chosen him before the foundation of the world. God selected those who would be in the Body of Christ before the world began.

a) Its concept

(1) The paradox

I believe in the doctrine of election because it is taught in the Bible. Scripture teaches that God chooses people to be saved before they're born and places their names in the book of life. That doesn't mean He violates man's will. The mystery of salvation is that although God elects people, they are at the same time responsible for their decisions. Jesus said, "Him that cometh to me I will in no wise cast out" (John 6:37). He also said, "Come unto me, all ye that labor and are heavy laden, and I will give you rest" (Matthew 11:28).

The paradox of divine election and human decision can be reconciled only in the mind of God. It's not our responsibility to resolve it. We must allow God to be sovereign.

(2) The purpose

In Ephesians 1:4 the Greek word translated "chosen" (*eklegō*) is in the aorist tense and middle voice, indicating God's totally independent choice. Because the verb is reflexive, it signifies that God not only chose *by* Himself but *for* Himself. Verse 6 tells us the reason: election is "to the praise of the glory of his grace." Verse 12 says, "We should be to the praise of his glory." And verse 14 ends with the phrase "unto the praise of his glory." Ephesians 3:10 tells us that God established the church to display His wisdom to the angels.

(3) The period

In Ephesians 1:4 Paul tells we were chosen "before the foundation of the world."

(a) Revelation 13:8—"All that dwell upon the earth shall worship [the Beast], whose names are not written in the book of life . . . from the foundation of the world."

(b) Revelation 17:8—"They that dwell on the earth shall wonder, whose names were not written in the book of life from the foundation of the world."

(4) The participants

(a) Israel—God didn't set His love upon Israel because it was the most righteous of all nations. Rather, He chose it because of the counsel of His own will. In Isaiah 45:4 God speaks of Israel as "mine elect."

(b) Angels—First Timothy 5:21 refers to "the elect angels."

(c) Jesus Christ—First Peter 2:6 says, "Behold, I lay in Zion a chief cornerstone, elect, precious."

(d) The apostles—Jesus said to the apostles, "Ye have not chosen me, but I have chosen you" (John 15:16). Christ referred to Paul as "a chosen vessel unto me, to bear my name before the Gentiles" (Acts 9:15).

(e) The church—Consistent with His nature, God chose the church before the foundation of the world.

(5) The plan

(a) 2 Timothy 1:9—God "hath saved us, and called us with an holy calling, not according to our works." Our election had nothing to do with what we did or didn't do, or with what God anticipated we would or would not do. We were chosen according to His own purpose and grace. Our physical and spiritual births were according to the divine plan of God.

(b) 2 Timothy 2:10—Paul said, "I endure all things for the elect's sake, that they may also obtain the salvation which is in Christ Jesus with eternal glory." Paul directed his ministry to reach those whom God had chosen.

(c) 2 Thessalonians 2:13—Paul wrote, "We are bound to give thanks always to God for you, brethren beloved of the Lord, because God hath from the beginning chosen you to salvation." We as believers were chosen before the foundation of the world.

(d) Acts 13:48—"When the Gentiles heard [the gospel], they were glad, and glorified the word of the Lord; and as many as were ordained to eternal life believed."

Conclusion

God formed His Body, which includes you if you're a Christian. Our worth comes from knowing that we are the object of God's choice. And because God has given us all spiritual blessings in the heavenlies, we have unlimited divine resources available to us. Be sure to use them to make your life fulfilling, to minister with the greatest amount of power, and to build the church that Jesus purchased with His precious blood. Because you are a child of the King, you are valuable to Him. As such, live so you might glorify Him.

Focusing on the Facts

1. Why does the body metaphor so aptly suit the church (see p. 24)?
2. When did God decide who would be in the Body of Christ (see p. 26)?
3. What is the biblical basis for self-worth (see p. 27)?
4. What does "blessed" mean in Ephesians 1:3 (see p. 28)?
5. What does it mean that God has blessed us with all spiritual blessings (see pp. 28-29)?
6. Why do Christians make unnecessary requests of God (Rom. 8:26; see p. 29)?
7. Where are our blessings located (Eph. 1:3; see p. 30)?
8. How does the believer's dual citizenship affect him (see p. 30)?
9. How would you describe Paul's outlook on life (2 Cor. 4:8-9; 6:10; see p. 31)?
10. How are spiritual resources appropriated (Gal. 5:22-23; see p. 31)?
11. What is the paradox in the fact that both sovereign election and human choice exist? How is that paradox ultimately resolved (see p. 32)?
12. Why did God choose us (1:4; see p. 33)?
13. When did election take place (see p. 33)?

Pondering the Principles

1. What is it that gives you your sense of self-worth or value? Read through the first chapter of Ephesians and write down all that you are and all that you've been given as a Christian. Next take some time to meditate on your list. Thank God for considering you valuable enough to bestow such riches upon you.

2. We are to praise God because He is good. What specific characteristics of God's goodness do the following verses teach: Psalm 145:8-9, 14-20; Matthew 5:45; John 3:16; Ephesians 2:4, 8-9; Titus 3:5; Hebrews 6:7; James 5:11; and 1 John 4:10?

3. Why do many Christians have such a difficult time believing both in God's sovereignty and man's responsibility? What does the Bible teach? Compare John 6:37a, 44, 65; Acts 13:48; and 2 Thessalonians 2:13; with John 6:35, 37b, 40, 47 and Revelation 22:17.

3
The Body Formed in Eternity Past—Part 2

Outline

Introduction
A. The Partnership of the Body
B. The Purpose for the Body
C. The Problem with the Body

Review
I. The Elements of the Blessing (v. 3)
II. The Eternal Formation of the Body (vv. 4-14)
   A. In the Past—Election (vv. 4-6a)
      1. The method: sovereign selection (v. 4a)
        a) Its concept

Lesson
        b) Its categories
          (1) Theocratic election
          (2) Vocational election
          (3) Salvational election
        c) Its compelling force
        d) Its confusion
      2. The object: the elect (v. 4b)
      3. The time: eternity past (v. 4c)
        a) Matthew 25:34
        b) First Peter 1:19-20
        c) Ephesians 2:10
      4. The purpose: holiness (v. 4d)
      5. The motive: love (v. 4e)
      6. The result: sonship (v. 5a)
      7. The reason: glory (vv. 5b-6a)

A. The Partnership of the Body

We as Christians have a common source of life. We entered
into the Body the same way—through the sacrifice of Jesus
Christ. We possess the same divine nature (2 Pet. 1:4). We
are moving toward the same destiny—the kingdom of God
and eternal glory in heaven with Christ. We are one in a
marvelous and unique way.

The central theme of Ephesians is our oneness in Christ.
The ramifications of that truth are discussed in every chapter of this book. We are called the Body of Christ to emphasize our unity. As the body responds to the brain, so the
church is to respond to the Lord Jesus Christ.

The unity of the church is based on the common life of its
members. The life of God pulses through the soul of every
believer. According to 1 Corinthians 6:17, "He that is joined
unto the Lord is one spirit." Therefore all who are joined to
the Lord are one with another.

Paul focused on theological matters in the first three chapters of Ephesians and on practical matters in the last three
chapters. He began the theological section with a look into
the past to view the divine plan of the church. There we
find that God the Father, Son, and Holy Spirit all had a part
in the planning of the church.

B. The Purpose for the Body

The best one-verse definition of the church is in Ephesians
4:13: Coming together "in the unity of the faith, and of the
knowledge of the Son of God, unto a perfect man, unto the
measure of the stature of the fullness of Christ." We enter
the Body of Christ by believing the same basic truths (i.e.,
"the unity of the faith," and "the knowledge of the Son of
God"). And we are progressing toward "the measure of the
stature of the fullness of Christ."

God's purpose for the Body is that it manifest Christ to the
world. God manifested Himself through the incarnation of

His Son (Body I) and the establishment of the church (Body II).

C. The Problem with the Body

The Body depends on the proper functioning of each of its parts. Therefore, when just one Christian sins, the corporate testimony of the Body is hindered. When someone doesn't function in the area of his spiritual giftedness, or follow through on his responsibilities of fellowship, he cripples the Body. Consequently, the world will receive a distorted picture of what Christ is like.

It's essential that we understand that we are one in Christ. Only when we understand the theology of the first half of Ephesians will we be prepared to apply the principles of Christian living in the second half of the book.

Review

I. THE ELEMENTS OF THE BLESSING (v. 3; see pp. 27-31)

"Blessed be the God and Father of our Lord Jesus Christ, who hath blessed us with all spiritual blessings in heavenly places in Christ."

II. THE ETERNAL FORMATION OF THE BODY (vv. 4-14; see pp. 32-35)

A. In the Past—Election (vv. 4-6a)

Some of God's ways we will never understand as fully as others, for "the secret things belong unto the Lord" (Deut. 29:29). Isaiah 55:9 tells us that God's ways are higher than man's ways.

1. The method: sovereign selection (v. 4a)

"According as he hath chosen."

a) Its concept (see pp. 32-35)

Lesson

God formed the Body in eternity past by independent, sovereign choice. He chose who would become the members of His Body—totally apart from any human consideration and purely on the basis of His own will. Paul wrote that we were chosen "according to the good pleasure of his will" (Eph. 1:5), "according to his good pleasure which he hath purposed in himself" (v. 9), and "according to the purpose of him who worketh all things after the counsel of his own will" (v. 11). God freely and independently chose us to be included in His Body—the church.

John spoke of Israel's rejection of the Messiah: "He came unto his own, and his own received him not. But as many as received him, to them gave he power to become the children of God, even to them that believe on his name; who were born, not of blood, nor of the will of the flesh, nor of the will of man, but of God" (1:11-13). Salvation is of God. Paul emphasizes that point in Ephesians 2:8-9: "By grace are ye saved through faith; and that not of yourselves, it is the gift of God." Second Timothy 1:9 tells us that God "saved us, and called us with an holy calling, not according to our works, but according to his own purpose and grace, which was given us in Christ before the world began."

Yet the Bible also teaches that man is responsible for his decisions. Jesus said, "Ye will not come to me, that ye might have life" (John 5:40). Isaiah said, "Every one that thirsteth, come to the waters, and he that hath no money; come, buy and eat; yea, come, buy wine and milk without money and without price" (55:1). In the book of Revelation John says, "The Spirit and the bride say, Come. And let him that heareth say, Come. And let him that is athirst come. And whosoever will, let him take the water of life freely" (22:17). Likewise, Paul claimed that "whosoever shall call upon the name of the Lord shall be saved" (Rom. 10:13).

So although the Bible holds out salvation to "whosoever will," it also teaches that salvation is a sovereign act of God. Only God can completely resolve that paradox.

Sovereignty: An Essential Christian Doctrine

1. God is the giver of all good things in general

We pray to God because we believe that He is the source of all good things. James said, "Every good gift and every perfect gift is from above, and cometh down from the Father of lights, with whom is no variableness, neither shadow of turning" (1:17). In prayer the Christian humbly acknowledges his dependence on God. Our health and daily provisions are a gift from God. That's why Jesus told us to pray "Give us this day our daily bread" (Matt. 6:11).

2. God is the giver of salvation in particular

We do not save ourselves—God saved us. Therefore we do not boast of our own merit, as though that resulted in our salvation. We thank God for saving us because we know that He alone caused it. We also bring our loved ones before Him in prayer because we realize that He alone saves them. Our prayers are a reminder that God is sovereign.

J. I. Packer said, "What is true is that all Christians believe in divine sovereignty, but some are not aware that they do, and mistakenly imagine and insist that they reject it. What causes this odd state of affairs? The root cause is the same as in most cases of error in the Church—the intruding of rationalistic speculations, the passion for systematic consistency, and reluctance to recognize the existence of mystery and to let God be wiser than men, and a consequent subjecting of Scripture to the supposed demands of human logic" (*Evangelism and the Sovereignty of God* [Downers Grove, Ill.: Inter-Varsity, 1961], p. 16).

Packer says that people basically can't tolerate tension in their thinking. People don't like to entertain the possibility of paradoxes or antinomy. Therefore they contrive a scheme to harmonize two truths and in effect destroy both by oversimplification.

Packer continues, "People see that the Bible teaches man's responsibility for his actions; they do not see . . . how this is consistent with the sovereign Lordship of God over those actions. They are not content to let the two truths live side by side, as they do in the Scriptures, but jump to the conclusion that, in order to uphold the biblical truth of human responsibility, they are bound to reject the equally biblical and equally true doctrine of divine sovereignty, and to explain away the great number of texts that teach it. The desire to over-simplify the Bible by cutting out the mysteries is natural to our perverse minds, and it is not surprising that even good men should fall victim to it. Hence this persistent and troublesome dispute. The irony of the situation, however, is that when we ask how the two sides pray, it becomes apparent that those who profess to deny God's sovereignty really believe in it just as strongly as those who affirm it" (pp. 16-17).

The Bible teaches that God chose everyone who is saved and that man is responsible for his decisions.

b) Its categories

(1) Theocratic election

Israel was once a theocracy—a nation ruled by God. Deuteronomy 7:6 says, "Thou art an holy people unto the Lord thy God; the Lord thy God hath chosen thee to be a special people unto himself, above all people who are upon the face of the earth." God didn't choose the biggest or the best—He chose freely out of love and grace.

However, just because a person was Jewish didn't mean that he was one of the elect. Paul said, "They are not all Israel, who are of Israel" (Rom. 9:6). As the biblical history of Israel demonstrates, being a part of the nation of Israel didn't guarantee that any individual experienced personal salvation.

(2) Vocational election

Sometimes God chooses certain people to do specific tasks. For instance, in Deuteronomy 18 God

42

chooses the Levites for a specific task—to function as the priestly tribe of Israel. Yet, because a person was a Levite did not automatically mean he was saved.

In the New Testament Jesus chose the twelve apostles to perform a task. However, Judas was not a believer. Jesus said to the apostles, "Ye have not chosen me, but I have chosen you" (John 15:16). The choosing in that verse was not for salvation but for the special task of being an apostle.

(3) Salvational election

God has chosen some to salvation. In Romans 16:13 Paul writes, "Greet Rufus, chosen in the Lord." God ordained that Rufus should be one of His children. Peter wrote his first epistle "to the sojourners scattered throughout Pontus, Galatia, Cappadocia, Asia, and Bithynia, elect according to the foreknowledge of God" (1:1-2). God chooses individuals to salvation.

c) Its compelling force

In John 6:44 Jesus says, "No man can come to me, except the Father, who hath sent me, draw him." No one is saved unless he is drawn (Gk., *helkō*). That term is used in nonbiblical writings to speak of an irresistible force. For example, it is used of a hungry man being drawn to food and of the power of love that draws two people together.

The force of God is like an electromagnet that draws iron while leaving nonferrous metal unmoved. God's election is irresistible to those upon whom He has set His love.

The elect of God inevitably respond in faith. Jesus said, "All that the Father giveth me shall come to me; and him that cometh to me I will in no wise cast out" (John 6:37). Romans 9 tells us that Jacob and Esau were chosen before they were born, so they obviously had nothing to do with their salvation. But in Romans

43

10 Paul says, "Whosoever shall call upon the name of the Lord shall be saved" (v. 13).

The hymn entitled "The Inner Life," written in 1904 by an unknown author, begins,

> I sought the Lord, and afterward I knew
> He moved my soul to seek Him, seeking me;
> It was not I that found, O Savior true;
> No, I was found of Thee.

d) Its confusion

Some are quick to point out that God's election was based on foreknowledge (cf. Rom. 8:28-29). Yet they incorrectly define foreknowledge as God's looking ahead in time to see how people would respond to the gospel and electing the ones who would react favorably. But that isn't what the Bible teaches.

The Biblical Definition of Foreknowledge

In Scripture foreknowledge (Gk., *proginōskō*) implies an intimate love relationship.

1. Genesis 4:17—"Cain knew his wife; and she conceived, and bore Enoch" (cf. vv. 1, 25). That does not refer to Cain's knowledge of his wife's existence; it refers to their intimate, physical relationship that resulted in the conception of a child.

2. Luke 1:34—After an angel told Mary she would have a child, she replied, "How shall this be, seeing I know not a man?" She meant that she had never had a sexual relationship with a man (cf. Matt. 1:25).

3. John 10:27—Jesus said, "My sheep hear my voice, and I know them." Jesus doesn't merely know who His sheep are—He has an intimate relationship with them.

4. Matthew 7:22-23—Jesus said, "Many will say to me in that day, Lord, Lord. . . . Then will I profess unto them, I never knew you." Jesus had never been in close, intimate relationship with them.

44

5. Amos 3:2—God looked at Israel and said, "You only have I known of all the families of the earth." Israel was the only nation with whom God was in close, intimate relationship.

Foreknowledge simply is God's love relationship for us established before the world began.

2. The object: the elect (v. 4b)

"He hath chosen us in him."

From a human perspective no one enters heaven except those who willfully and consciously submit to God. Jesus said, "Ye will not come to me, that ye might have life" (John 5:40). In Luke 22 we see God's sovereignty and the will of man placed side by side: "Truly the Son of man goeth, as it was determined; but woe unto that man by whom he is betrayed!" (v. 22). God was sovereign, but Judas was responsible for each of his deeds. The sovereignty of God does not nullify man's responsibility.

3. The time: eternity past (v. 4c)

"Before the foundation of the world."

That is known as predestination: We were chosen by God before the creation of the universe.

a) Matthew 25:34—A day is coming when Christ will proclaim, "Come, ye blessed of my Father, inherit the kingdom prepared for you from the foundation of the world."

b) First Peter 1:19-20—Peter said we were redeemed "with the precious blood of Christ, as of a lamb without blemish and without spot, who verily was foreordained before the foundation of the world." Christ's crucifixion was planned out before the world began.

c) Ephesians 2:10—"We are his workmanship, created in Christ Jesus unto good works, which God hath before ordained that we should walk in them."

45

4. The purpose: holiness (v. 4*d*)

"That we should be holy and without blame [Gk., *amō-mos*, "without blemish"] before him."

We are holy before God because Christ's holiness has been imputed to us. That is why we say that Christians have positional holiness—their position being in Christ. Paul addressed such holiness in its application to the church: "A glorious church, not having spot, or wrinkle, or any such thing; but that it should be holy and without blemish" (Eph. 5:27). The death of Christ covers our sin, and His righteousness is reckoned to our account. So we have been reconciled to God by the substitutionary death of Christ.

Before God we are as holy as Jesus—that's our position. But we know that's not our practice. We are far from the holy standard and far from being blameless. Yet in Colossians 2:9-10 Paul says, "In him [Christ] dwelleth all the fullness of the Godhead bodily. And ye are complete in him." All that God is we become in Jesus Christ. That's why salvation is secure. We have Christ's perfect righteousness. Our practice can and does fall short, but our position can never fall short, because it is the same holy and blameless position Christ has before God. We are as secure as our Savior because we are in Him. And because God has declared us to be holy and blameless, we should strive to reflect that in our lives.

5. The motive: love (v. 4*e*)

"In love."

God chose us to be His children because of His love (John 3:16). Love is what motivated God to extend mercy to unworthy man. Love is not an emotion; it's an act of self-sacrifice on behalf of others. The preeminent expression of God's love is the death of His Son: "Greater love hath no man than this, that a man lay down his life for his friends" (John 15:13). And God set His love upon us before the world began.

Love is an attribute of God—"God is love" (1 John 4:8). His love for men precedes their love for God (1 John 4:19). Ephesians 2:4-5 says, "God, who is rich in mercy, for his great love with which he loved us . . . hath made us alive together with Christ."

6. The result: sonship (v. 5a)

"Having predestinated us unto the adoption of sons by Jesus Christ himself."

We have been adopted by God because we are in Christ. In Christ we became subjects of His kingdom, and because He is our Lord we are His servants. He even calls us friends (John 15:15). But in His great love He makes us more than citizens and servants, and even more than friends. He makes us children, lovingly drawing us into the intimacy of His own family.

We became His children the same instant we were saved (John 1:12). In fact, as His children we can now address God in an intimate way—"Abba," the Aramaic equivalent of "Daddy" (Gal. 4:6). Our adoption means that the life of God dwells in us. Human parents can adopt children and love them as much as they do their natural children. But no human parent can impart his own distinct nature to an adopted child. Yet that is exactly what God has done for us. We are "partakers of the divine nature" (2 Pet. 1:4) in that the Spirit of God dwells in us (Gal. 4:6).

7. The reason: glory (vv. 5b-6a)

"According to the good pleasure of his will, to the praise of the glory of his grace."

All creation exists to bring glory to God. In Isaiah 43 God says, "The beasts of the field will glorify Me" (v. 20, NASB). Psalm 19 says, "The heavens declare the glory of God" (v. 1). The only rebels in the universe are fallen angels and fallen men. Everything else glorifies its Creator. The fallen angels have already been eternally removed from God's presence, and so will the fallen people who refuse to be saved by Jesus Christ. In fact, Paul said that everything we do is to be "to the glory of God" (1 Cor. 10:31).

God chose certain people to be in the Body of Christ that He might be glorified. Salvation is all from God and therefore all the glory goes to Him. To guarantee that, every provision of salvation was accomplished before any human being was ever born. Jesus told His disciples, "It is your Father's good pleasure to give you the kingdom" (Luke 12:32). He fit us into the Body of Christ to be the praise of His glory.

Focusing on the Facts

1. What is God's purpose for the Body of Christ (see p. 38)?
2. When we fail to exercise our spiritual gifts, how does it affect the testimony of the church (see p. 39)?
3. When did God form the Body of Christ (Eph. 1:4; see p. 40)?
4. On what basis did God choose us to become members of the Body of Christ (see p. 40)?
5. What is the "gift of God" referred to in Ephesians 2:8-9 (see p. 40)?
6. Give three passages from the Bible that show that all people are responsible to make their own choice (see p. 40).
7. Why can it be said that our prayers acknowledge the sovereignty of God (see p. 41)?
8. According to J. I. Packer, why do people have such a difficult time accepting both truths of man's responsibility and God's sovereignty (see pp. 41-42)?
9. Name and define the three kinds of election mentioned in the Bible (see pp. 42-43).
10. How does John 6:44 shed light on the paradox of divine sovereignty and human choice (see p. 43)?
11. How is foreknowledge defined in Scripture (see pp. 44-45)?
12. According to Ephesians 1:4, what is the purpose of our election (see p. 46)?
13. What does 1 John 4:19 tell us about our love of God (see p. 47)?
14. What does it mean that we are adopted by God (1 Pet. 1:4; Gal. 4:6; see p. 47)?

15. What does Isaiah 43:20 tell us about the created universe (see p. 47)?

Pondering the Principles

1. As members of the Body of Christ, we all have certain responsibilities to one another. Look up the following verses and write down the "one anothers" we are to be practicing: Galatians 5:13; 6:1-2; Ephesians 4:32; 5:21; Colossians 3:16; 1 Thessalonians 4:18; 5:11; Hebrews 3:13; James 5:16; 1 Peter 1:22; 4:9-10. List the "one anothers" on a sheet of paper beginning with the one that you believe is the least evident in your life. Talk about your list with your spouse or a close friend. Have that individual evaluate your order, giving you counsel as to what they perceive to be your strengths and weaknesses.

2. Ephesians 1:4 tells us we are holy by virtue of our position in Christ. According to 1 Peter 1:15-16, 2 Peter 3:14, and 1 John 3:7, how are we to live in light of our position? What are the specific areas you need to work on to make you more set apart (holy) from sin unto God?

4
Redemption Through His Blood

Outline

Introduction
A. Redemption Characterized
  1. The definition
  2. The different terms
    a) *Agorazō / exagorazō*
    b) *Lutroō / apolutrōsis*
  3. The deliverance
    a) The captivity of sin
      (1) John 8:34
      (2) Romans 6:17
      (3) Romans 7:14
      (4) Romans 8:21
    b) The consequence of sin
      (1) Romans 6:23
      (2) Hebrews 9:22
      (3) Ezekiel 18:20
    c) The conqueror of sin
      (1) Galatians 5:1
      (2) Galatians 1:3-4
      (3) Colossians 1:13
      (4) Romans 6:18
      (5) Galatians 3:13
      (6) Hebrews 2:14-15
B. Redemption Compared
  1. Defined
    a) Justification (Gk., *dikaiōsis*)
    b) Forgiveness (Gk., *aphesis*)
    c) Adoption (Gk., *huiothesia*)
    d) Reconciliation (Gk., *katalassō*)
    e) Redemption (Gk., *apolutrōsis*)

2. Distinguished
   a) Justification
   b) Forgiveness
   c) Adoption
   d) Reconciliation
   e) Redemption

Review
I. The Blessing's Elements (v. 3)
II. The Body's Eternal Formation (vv. 4-14)
   A. In the Past—Election (vv. 4-6*a*)

Lesson
   B. In the Present—Redemption (vv. 6*b*-10)
      1. The redeemer (vv. 6*b*-7*a*)
         a) His ascription
            (1) Mark 1:11
            (2) Mark 9:7
            (3) Colossians 1:13
         b) Our acceptance
      2. The redeemed (vv. 6*b*-7*a*)
         a) Ephesians 2:1-3
         b) Ephesians 2:11-12
         c) Ephesians 4:17-19
      3. The redemption (v. 7*b*)
         a) Its proper meaning
         b) Its permanent effectiveness
         c) Its perceived value
            (1) 1 Peter 1:18-19
            (2) Revelation 5:9-12
      4. The results (vv. 7*c*-8)
         a) Forgiveness (v. 7*c*)
            (1) Its portrayal
            (2) Its origin
            (3) Its extent
               (*a*) Psalm 103:12
               (*b*) Isaiah 44:22
               (*c*) Micah 7:18-19
            (4) Its perpetuation
            (5) Its abundance

 b) Wisdom and prudence (v. 8)
  (1) Distinguished
   (a) Wisdom (Gk., *sophia*)
   (b) Prudence (Gk., *phronēsis*)
  (2) Displayed
 5. The reason (vv. 9-10)

Introduction

A. Redemption Characterized

 1. The definition

  In redemption God Himself pays the ransom or price for sin. Redemption is deliverance by the payment of a price.

 2. The different terms

  a) Agorazō / exagorazō—Both those words are translated "redemption" in the New Testament. The Greek root of both is *agora*, which means "marketplace."

  b) Lutroō / apolutrōsis—The Greek word translated "redemption" in Ephesians 1:7 (*apolutrōsis*) is an intensified form of *lutroō*, which refers to paying a price to free someone from bondage. During New Testament times the Roman Empire had approximately 20 million slaves, and buying and selling slaves was a major business. If a person wanted to free a loved one or friend who was a slave, he would buy the slave for himself and then grant him freedom. He would testify to that deliverance by a written certificate. *Lutroō* was used to designate such a transaction.

 3. The deliverance

  a) The captivity of sin

  We are all born in the state of slavery—everyone is held captive by sin from birth.

(1) John 8:34—Jesus said, "Whosoever committeth sin is the servant of sin" (cf. Eccles. 7:20).

(2) Romans 6:17—Paul described the Roman Christians as "the servants of sin" before they were saved.

(3) Romans 7:14—Paul also said that he was "sold under sin."

(4) Romans 8:21—In the future, creation will be "delivered from the bondage of corruption."

b) The consequence of sin

Sin demands a price be paid.

(1) Romans 6:23—Ultimately the price that must be paid is death: "The wages of sin is death."

(2) Hebrews 9:22—"Without shedding of blood [imagery of a violent death] is no remission [of sins]."

(3) Ezekiel 18:20—"The soul that sinneth, it shall die."

c) The conqueror of sin

Jesus redeemed us by paying the price sin required.

(1) Galatians 5:1—"It was for freedom that Christ set us free" (NASB).

(2) Galatians 1:3-4—"Our Lord Jesus Christ . . . gave himself for our sins, that he might deliver us from this present evil age."

(3) Colossians 1:13—God "hath delivered us from the power of darkness, and hath translated us into the kingdom of his dear Son."

(4) Romans 6:18—"Being, then, made free from sin, ye became the servants of righteousness."

(5) Galatians 3:13—"Christ hath redeemed us from the curse of the law, being made a curse for us."

(6) Hebrews 2:14-15—"As the children are partakers of flesh and blood, he also himself likewise took part of the same [i.e., God became a man], that through death he might destroy him that had the power of death, that is, the devil, and deliver them who, through fear of death, were all their lifetime subject to bondage."

B. Redemption Compared

Five Greek legal terms help us understand redemption.

1. Defined

   a) Justification (Gk., *dikaiōsis*)

   Justification refers to acquittal in a court of law.

   b) Forgiveness (Gk., *aphesis*)

   Forgiveness speaks of a canceled debt. Whenever a debt was canceled, retribution made, or the price paid, the word *aphesis* was used.

   c) Adoption (Gk., *huiothesia*)

   Adoption refers to the legal process of going to court to accept a child as one's own. The Bible uses that term to speak of sonship—of becoming a son of God.

   d) Reconciliation (Gk., *katallassō*)

   Reconciliation was used to indicate that peace had been made between two warring parties (e.g., 2 Cor. 5:20).

   e) Redemption (Gk., *apolutrōsis*)

   Redemption refers to purchasing a prisoner for the purpose of setting him free.

2. Distinguished

    a) Justification—the sinner stands before God accused but is declared righteous because of his position in Christ (Rom. 8:33).

    b) Forgiveness—the sinner stands before God as a debtor, but his obligation brought by sin is canceled (Eph. 1:7).

    c) Adoption—the sinner stands before God as a stranger but is made a son (Eph. 1:5).

    d) Reconciliation—the sinner stands before God as an enemy but is made a friend (2 Cor. 5:18-20).

    e) Redemption—the sinner stands before God as a slave but receives freedom (Rom. 6:18-22).

All those terms are different facets of the magnificent diamond of the doctrine of salvation. Redemption is just one facet of our salvation.

Review

I. THE BLESSING'S ELEMENTS (v. 3; see pp. 27-31)

II. THE BODY'S ETERNAL FORMATION (vv. 4-14)

    A. In the Past—Election (vv. 4-6*a*; see pp. 32-35, 40-48)

Lesson

    B. In the Present—Redemption (vv. 6*b*-10)

        1. The redeemer (vv. 6*b*-7*a*)

        "Through [grace] he hath made us accepted in the beloved; in whom we have redemption."

Our Redeemer is "the Beloved"—Jesus Christ. We are acceptable to God because we have been made one with Christ through faith. In Him we are made acceptable and given redemption.

a) His ascription

The term *Beloved* was God's special name for His Son.

(1) Mark 1:11—When Jesus was baptized the Father spoke from heaven, saying, "Thou art my beloved Son, in whom I am well pleased."

(2) Mark 9:7—At the transfiguration the Father again spoke from heaven, saying, "This is my beloved Son; hear him."

(3) Colossians 1:13—Paul tells us that God has "transferred us to the kingdom of His beloved Son" (NASB).

b) Our acceptance

God gives His abundant riches to Christ, and because we are in Christ, we are recipients as well. Christ is accepted by the Father, and we are accepted because of our relationship to His Son.

The Greek word translated "accepted" in Ephesians 1:6 means "graced." We could translate Ephesians 1:6, "We have been graced by God's grace." God extends His grace to us because we are in Christ.

2. The redeemed (vv. 6*b*-7*a*)

The redeemed are referred to as "us" (v. 6) and "we" (v. 7). But who exactly are the redeemed?

a) Ephesians 2:1-3—"You . . . were dead in trespasses and sins; in which in times past ye walked according to the course of this world, according to the prince of the power of the air [Satan], the spirit that now worketh in the sons of disobedience; among whom also we all had our manner of life in times past in the lusts of our flesh, fulfilling the desires of the flesh and of the mind, and were by nature the children of wrath, even as others."

b) Ephesians 2:11-12—"Remember that ye, being in time past Gentiles . . . without Christ, being aliens from the commonwealth of Israel, and strangers from the covenants of promise, having no hope, and without God in the world."

c) Ephesians 4:17-19—"Ye henceforth walk not as other Gentiles walk, in the vanity of their mind, having the understanding darkened, being alienated from the life of God through the ignorance that is in them, because of the blindness of their heart; who, being past feeling, have given themselves over unto lasciviousness, to work all uncleanness with greediness."

The people God redeems are sinners. They were at one time lewd, greedy, blind, ignorant, alienated, and darkened, and were without hope because they were without God. In Titus 2 Paul says that Christ "gave himself for us that he might redeem us from all iniquity, and purify unto himself a people of his own, zealous of good works" (v. 14). Jesus said, "I am not come to call the righteous, but sinners to repentance" (Matt. 9:13). Before a person can be freed from the slavery of sin, he must acknowledge his sin. And as Paul says in Romans 3, "All have sinned, and come short of the glory of God" (v. 23).

3. The redemption (v. 7b)

"Redemption through his blood."

a) Its proper meaning

Romans 3:23 says, "The wages of sin is death." The price of sin is death. Someone had to die, and Jesus did. "His blood" is a metonym for the violent death of Christ on the cross. Through the shedding of His blood, Christ poured out His life as a sacrificial, sub-stitutionary payment for sin.

In the New Testament we find that Christ gave not only His blood (Acts 20:28) but also His very life (Matt. 20:28) and self (Gal. 1:4). Though stated differently, they all refer to the same thing—Christ's death on our behalf. Through the sacrifice of His Son God showed us mercy without violating His justice.

b) Its permanent effectiveness

The death of Christ purchased our redemption. The Old Testament sacrificial system was only symbolic of the coming death of the Lamb of God. Hebrews says, "By one offering he hath perfected forever them that are sanctified" (10:14).

c) Its perceived value

(1) 1 Peter 1:18-19—"Ye know that ye were not re-deemed with corruptible things, like silver and gold, from your vain manner of life received by tradition from your fathers, but with the precious blood of Christ."

(2) Revelation 5:9-12—"They sang a new song, say-ing, Thou art worthy to take the scroll, and to open its seals; for thou wast slain, and hast re-deemed us to God by thy blood out of every kin-dred, and tongue, and people, and nation; and hast made us unto our God a kingdom of priests, and we shall reign on the earth. . . . Worthy is the Lamb that was slain to receive power, and riches, and wisdom, and strength, and honor, and glory, and blessing."

The blood of Christ—emblematic of His sacrificial, sub-stitutionary death—frees us from the guilt of sin, the condemnation of sin, the power of sin, the penalty of sin, and will remove us from the presence of sin.

4. The results (vv. 7c-8)

a) Forgiveness (v. 7c)

"The forgiveness of sins, according to the riches of his grace."

Speaking to the disciples about the Lord's Supper, Christ said, "This is my blood of the new testament, which is shed for many for the remission [forgiveness] of sins" (Matt. 26:28).

(1) Its portrayal

Israel understood the concept of forgiveness in the Old Testament. On the Day of Atonement (Yom Kippur), the high priest sacrificed a goat and sprinkled its blood on the altar. Then he placed his hands on the head of another goat, confessed the people's sins over it, and sent it out into the wilderness where it could never find its way back. That goat symbolized forgiveness—sending sin where it could never be seen again. The Greek word translated "forgiveness" in Ephesians 1:7 (*aphesis*) means "to send away never to return."

(2) Its origin

Remember that the events described in the first chapter of Ephesians happened before the world began. Depressed Christians forget that God looked down the corridors of time even before He fashioned the earth and placed the sins of His elect on the head of His Son, who took them an eternal distance away. So our sins were forgiven before God created the universe.

(3) Its extent

(a) Psalm 103:12—"As far as the east is from the west, so far hath he removed our transgressions from us."

(b) Isaiah 44:22—"I have blotted out, like a thick cloud, thy transgressions, and, like a cloud, thy sins; return unto me; for I have redeemed thee."

(c) Micah 7:18-19—"Who is a God like unto thee, who pardoneth iniquity, and passeth by the transgression of the remnant of his heritage? He retaineth not his anger forever, because he delighteth in mercy. He will turn again; he will have compassion upon us; he will subdue our iniquities; and thou wilt cast all their sins into the depths of the sea."

Shakespeare's King Richard III said, "My conscience hath a thousand several tongues, and every tongue brings a several tale, and every tale condemns me" (Act V.iii.194-96). That isn't true of the believer. When Jesus comes into our lives, He tells us what He told the woman at the well, "Neither do I condemn thee; go, and sin no more" (John 8:11). In Romans 8:1 Paul says, "There is . . . now no condemnation to them who are in Christ." Our sins have been forgiven—not because we deserve it but because of Christ's sacrifice on our behalf.

Are You Responsible?

One school of thought in modern psychology undermines personal responsibility in wrongdoing. Its adherents claim that we are merely victims of our past in an attempt to remove personal guilt. Although their intentions are good, in the end they do mankind a disservice, because we all have an emotional, psychological, and spiritual need to acknowledge guilt.

The gospel clearly declares the guilt of mankind. All people are personally responsible for their sins. However, the gospel also proclaims good news: that Christ paid the penalty for our sins for us. He suffered to set us free. The Bible presents the only effective prescription for guilt: forgiveness. It is available to all who receive it. The apostle John said, "I write unto you, little children, because

61

your sins are forgiven you for his name's sake" (1 John 2:12). Ephesians 4:32 says, "Be ye kind one to another, tenderhearted, forgiving one another, even as God, for Christ's sake, hath forgiven you." And Colossians 2:13 says, "You, being dead in your sins . . . hath he [God] made alive together with him [Christ], having forgiven you all trespasses."

(4) Its perpetuation

God did not forgive only our past sins. Christ paid for all our sins—past, present, and future. Jesus said to Peter that once a person has had a bath (being saved), all he needs is to wash his feet when they become dusty (confess his sins; John 13:10). First John 1:9 says, "If we confess our sins, he is faithful and just to forgive us our sins, and to cleanse us from all unrighteousness." That is how we are to deal with sin on a day-to-day basis.

Why the Lingering Sense of Guilt?

We are accepted by God because of our union with Christ. In fact, those who receive Christ are the children of God (John 1:12). Yet many believers continue to feel guilt or inferiority because they don't have an adequate understanding of God.

Name droppers boast that they are friends with famous people. However, a Christian can legitimately boast that the God of the universe is his friend. In fact, Christ is now in heaven preparing a place for the believer to spend eternity (John 14:1-3). In addition, God has granted him everything he needs (2 Pet. 1:3).

Many times a believer's low view of himself is caused by his failure to understand his position in Christ. As believers, our worth is based upon the worth of God's Son. Because of Christ, we have value to God. Because of Christ, we should value ourselves and others.

(5) Its abundance

God's forgiveness is "according to the riches of his grace" (v. 7). God's grace is boundless. It is far beyond our ability to comprehend or describe, yet we know it is "according to the riches" of that infinite grace that He provides forgiveness. If you were to ask a millionaire to contribute to a worthy ministry, and he gave you a check for twenty-five dollars, he would only be giving *out of* his riches. But if he gave you a check for twenty-five thousand dollars, he would be giving *according to* his riches. God gives according to His riches, not out of His riches.

b) Wisdom and prudence (v. 8)

"In which he hath abounded toward us in all wisdom and prudence."

(1) Distinguished

(*a*) Wisdom (Gk., *sophia*)

Sophia frequently refers to wisdom in eternal things such as life, death, God, man, sin, and eternity. Its emphasis is on theological issues.

(*b*) Prudence (Gk., *phronēsis*)

Prudence often refers to insight into earthly things. Its emphasis is on practical living.

(2) Displayed

God forgives our sins and then gives us insight to live for Him in a hostile world. The modern French author André Maurois was a relativist and wrote a book on the subject. He believed the universe was indifferent, convinced that there was no way for anyone to attain total, absolute truth in any area, including creation. Yet the truth is that God has "hidden these things from the [self-proclaimed] wise and prudent, and hast revealed them unto babes" (Luke 10:21). James said, "If any of you lack wisdom, let him ask of God, who giveth to all men liberally, and upbraideth not, and it shall be given him" (1:5).

5. The reason (vv. 9-10)

"Having made known unto us the mystery of his will, according to his good pleasure which he hath purposed in himself; that in the dispensation of the fullness of times he might gather together in one all things in Christ, both which are in heaven, and which are in earth, even in him."

At the completion of history, when the millennial kingdom is phased into the eternal state, God will gather together all the redeemed. At that time "every knee should bow, of things in heaven, and things in earth, and things under the earth, and that every tongue should confess that Jesus Christ is Lord, to the glory of God, the Father" (Phil. 2:10-11). Christ will gather the entire universe into unity (Ps. 2; Heb. 1:8-13). At the present time the universe is anything but unified. It is corrupted, divided, and splintered. Although Satan rules the world now, God will cast him and his demons into the lake of fire (Rev. 20:10).

When God has disposed of every trace of evil, He will establish an incomparable unity in Himself of the things that remain. That is the inevitable goal of the universe.

Shakespeare's Macbeth said that life is "a tale told by an idiot, full of sound and fury, signifying nothing" (Act V.v.23-27). That statement is not true. God has an absolutely clear and wonderful purpose in mind, and at the completion of history He will bring all things together to Himself.

Focusing on the Facts

1. Define redemption (see p. 53).
2. Redemption delivers us from the bondage of what (see p. 53)?
3. What price was paid to release us from sin's grasp (see p. 54)?
4. What are five legal terms used in the New Testament to describe the different facets of salvation (see p 55)?
5. How do those five terms differ from each other (see p. 56)?
6. What name is used to identify our Redeemer in Ephesians 1:6? Why (see p. 57)?
7. What makes an individual acceptable to God? Explain (see p. 57).
8. What characteristic is common to all the redeemed (see p. 58)?
9. What purchased our redemption (v. 7; see pp. 58-59)?
10. What did the Old Testament sacrifices symbolize (see p. 59)?
11. What are the results of redemption (vv. 7-8; see pp. 60, 63)?
12. How did the Day of Atonement picture redemption for the nation of Israel (see p. 60)?
13. When were our sins forgiven (see p. 60)?
14. Explain the difference between wisdom and prudence (see p. 63).
15. Why did God redeem us (see p. 64)?

Pondering the Principles

1. Read Romans 6:16-22. Are Christians and non-Christians free to live as they please? Explain your answer using Paul's teaching in this text. Believers have been set free from bondage to sin. Does any part of your life reflect that you are still living as though you're under bondage? After you have confessed and repented of that sin, seek out another believer to whom you can be accountable.

2. Read 1 Corinthians 6:9-11. The gospel has the power to transform even the most wicked of men and women. Yet sometimes we think that some people are beyond the power of God. But remember, every soul that is saved is a miracle because everyone is a sinner in God's sight. This week pray for God to do such a miracle in the life of someone you know.

3. Even though all your sins have been forgiven, it is important to confess your sins before God. What do the following passages teach about the importance of confession: Psalm 32:1-5, 38:17-18, 66:18, Prov. 28:13-14, and 1 Corinthians 11:23-32? Why is confession important before you study God's Word?

5
Divine Promises Guaranteed

Outline

Introduction
A. The Integrity of God's Promises
   1. 2 Peter 3:9
   2. Titus 1:2
   3. Hebrews 10:23
   4. Romans 4:21
B. The Identification of God's Promises
   1. The double meaning of our inheritance
     a) We are Christ's inheritance
       (1) Presented by the Father
       (2) Purchased by Christ
         (*a*) 1 Corinthians 6:19-20
         (*b*) Acts 20:28
     b) Christ is our inheritance
   2. The description of our inheritance

Review
I. The Elements of the Blessing (v. 3)
II. The Eternal Formation of the Body (vv. 4-14)
   A. In the Past—Election (vv. 4-6*a*)
   B. In the Present—Redemption (vv. 6*b*-10)

Lesson
   C. In the Future—Inheritance (vv. 11-14)
     1. The ground of our inheritance (vv. 11-13*a*)
       a) The fact of our union with Christ (v. 11*a*)
       b) The cause of our union with Christ (vv. 11*b*-13*a*)

      (1) From the divine perspective (vv. 11b-12a)
         (a) Predetermination (v. 11b)
         (b) Power (v. 11c)
         (c) Preeminence (v. 12a)
      (2) From the human perspective (vv. 12b-13a)
         (a) The unresolved question
         (b) The ultimate response
  2. The guarantee of our inheritance (vv. 13b-14a)
    a) The seal (v. 13b)
      (1) A sign of security
      (2) A sign of authenticity
      (3) A sign of a completed transaction
      (4) A sign of authority
    b) The guarantee (v. 14a)
  3. The goal of our inheritance (v. 14b)

Introduction

Through the years I've had many conversations with young and old alike who face life with a foreboding sense of unfulfillment. They wonder if life has the potential to be wonderful and exciting. Ephesians 1:11-14 speaks to that issue. Life can be meaningful and fulfilling because of the promises God has for those who are in Christ.

A. The Integrity of God's Promises

It is easy to be cynical whenever someone makes a promise. We've all known people who made promises and didn't keep them—and we've all made promises we didn't keep. Our society is full of promises, albeit broken promises. Governments make promises and break them. Advertisers make promises and break them. Preachers make promises and break them. Husbands, wives, brothers, sisters, moms, dads, aunts, uncles, friends, and enemies make promises and break them. But there is One who makes promises and never breaks them.

1. 2 Peter 3:9—"The Lord is not slack concerning his promise."

2. Titus 1:2—"God . . . cannot lie."

3. Hebrews 10:23—"He who promised is faithful" (NIV*).

4. Romans 4:21—"What he had promised, he was able also to perform."

B. The Identification of God's Promises

1. The double meaning of our inheritance

Ephesians 1:11 begins, "In whom also we have obtained an inheritance." The Greek verb translated "have obtained" is in the past tense. There are two possible translations that result in two different meanings.

a) We are Christ's inheritance

The passive verb could be translated, "In whom we were made an inheritance." That would mean we are Christ's inheritance—He inherited us. Even if that is not what Paul intended this verse to mean, it still is a true statement.

(1) Presented by the Father

Jesus said, "All that the Father giveth me shall come to me" (John 6:37). We are a gift from the Father to the Son. That's the sense in which we are His inheritance. Malachi 3:17 says, "They shall be mine, saith the Lord of hosts, in that day when I make up my jewels."

God granted the church to His Son as a reward for His faithfulness. Because of Jesus' crucifixion and resurrection, "God also hath highly exalted him, and given him a name which is above every name, that at the name of Jesus every knee should bow" (Phil. 2:9-10). God not only exalted Jesus because of His work on the cross but also gave Him the spoils of His victory: us.

If you're struggling with a lack of self-worth, remember that you were important enough for God

New International Version.

to give you to Jesus as an inheritance. You're a love gift from the Father to the Son.

(2) Purchased by Christ

Christ bought us at the cross.

    (a) 1 Corinthians 6:19-20—Paul said to the Corinthians, "Know ye not that your body is the temple of the Holy Spirit who is in you, whom ye have of God, and ye are not your own? For ye are bought with a price."

    (b) Acts 20:28—Paul told the Ephesian elders, "He hath purchased [the church of God] with his own blood."

b) Christ is our inheritance

The King James Version translates Ephesians 1:11, "In whom also we have obtained an inheritance." So the passive verb can mean that we have received Christ as an inheritance. In one sense we are His inheritance; in another sense He is our inheritance. No matter which translation is appropriate to the exegesis of Ephesians 1:11, we know both are true because of what Paul says in 1 Corinthians 3:21-23: "All things are yours, whether Paul, or Apollos, or Cephas, or the world, or life, or death, or things present, or things to come; all are yours, and ye are Christ's." First he said all things are ours, then he said we are Christ's. We inherit everything, and He inherits us.

Are People Seeing Less of You and More of Christ?

First Corinthians 6:17 says, "He that is joined unto the Lord is one spirit." When you became a Christian you became one with Jesus Christ. In a sense you lose your identity because the Christian's identity is Christ. In Philippians 1:21 Paul says, "To me to live is Christ." That was his identity.

As Christians we are to be living examples of Christ to the world. We are to love like He loved, help like He helped, care like He cared, and share like He shared. God didn't put us in the world to take advantage of others; we're to serve others. So when a true Christian lives the way he ought to live, the world will see the reality of Christ in his life.

In the context of Ephesians 1, I believe Paul is emphasizing that Christ is our inheritance because he has been discussing the things God has given us (vv. 3-10).

2. The description of our inheritance

First Peter 1:4 says that because you were begotten in Christ, you have "an inheritance incorruptible, and undefiled, and that fadeth not away, reserved in heaven for you." Part of your inheritance is appropriated the moment you become a Christian, although the fulfillment of it is yet future.

Ours is a limitless inheritance. Second Peter 1:4 says we have been given "exceedingly great and precious promises." Second Corinthians 1:20 says, "All the promises of God in him [Christ] are yea, and in him Amen." All God's promises were made in behalf of those who belong to Christ.

Whatever you might be looking for, you can be sure God promised it. God has promised believers peace, love, grace, wisdom, eternal life, joy, victory, strength, guidance, provision for all our needs, power, knowledge, mercy, forgiveness, righteousness, gifts of the Spirit, fellowship with the Trinity, instruction from the Word, truth, spiritual discernment, and eternal riches, to name a few. When we became Christians we were made one with Jesus Christ. Therefore we receive everything the Father gives Him. Paul said we were made "heirs of God, and joint heirs with Christ" (Rom. 8:17).

Review

In Ephesians 1:3-14 Paul praises God for the wonderful promises He has made to us through Jesus Christ.

I. THE ELEMENTS OF THE BLESSING (v. 3; see pp. 27-31)

II. THE ETERNAL FORMATION OF THE BODY (vv. 4-14)

    A. In the Past—Election (vv. 4-6*a*; see pp. 32-35, 40-48)

    B. In the Present—Redemption (vv. 6*b*-10; see pp. 53-64)

Lesson

    C. In the Future—Inheritance (vv. 11-14)

There are three things I want you to see in this text: the ground of our inheritance, the guarantee of our inheritance, and the goal of our inheritance.

1. The ground of our inheritance (vv. 11-13*a*)

    a) The fact of our union with Christ (v. 11*a*)

"In whom [Christ] also we have obtained an inheritance."

The ground of our inheritance is Christ. There's no way to receive anything God has to offer apart from Christ. Acts 4:12 says, "Neither is there salvation in any other; for there is no other name under heaven given among men, whereby we must be saved." Our inheritance comes from being one with Christ. In fact, Ephesians 1:3 says we are blessed because we are in Christ.

The concept of our union with Christ is seen vividly in Romans 6:3-5. Paul said, "Know ye not that, as many of us as were baptized into Jesus Christ were baptized into his death? Therefore, we are buried with him by baptism into death, that as Christ was raised up from the dead by the glory of the Father, even so we also should walk in newness of life. For if we have been planted together in the likeness of his death, we shall be also in the likeness of his resurrection." When you became a Christian, in a sense you were transported back in time and nailed to the cross of Christ, buried with Him, and risen with Him. Now you are one with Christ forever. When you died with Him your sins were paid for. When you rose with Him you were enabled to live a new life. Now that you are one with Him you receive all the inheritance God could ever give His beloved Son.

Ultimately the wonder of all wonders is that someday when Jesus appears, we will be like Him (1 John 3:2). Romans 8:29 says God predestined us "to be conformed to the image of his Son." It's not that God loves us just enough to bring us into His family—He loves us so much that He makes us like His Son.

b) The cause of our union with Christ (vv. 11b-13a)

(1) From the divine perspective (vv. 11b-12a)

(a) Predetermination (v. 11b)

"Being predestinated according to the purpose of him."

God predetermined that we would obtain an inheritance in Christ. Ephesians 1:4 says, "He hath chosen us in him before the foundation of the world." That concept overwhelms me. I'll never understand why God would choose an inadequate, useless sinner like myself. But He predestinated each one of us according to His own purpose. The Greek word translated "predestinated" (proorizō) means "to mark out the boundaries." God planned out the salvation of each believer.

73

(*b*) Power (v. 11*c*)

"Who worketh all things after the counsel of his own will."

The Greek word translated "worketh" (*energeō*) is the origin for the English words *energetic*, *energize*, and *energy*. Whatever God plans, He energizes. He created the world simply by desiring to do so. Whatever He thinks is energized into reality because He is all powerful.

Since God in His grace chose us to be a part of His plan for eternity, He surely will bring it to pass. Paul said to be "confident of this very thing, that he who hath begun a good work in you will perform it until the day of Jesus Christ" (Phil. 1:6). What God starts He finishes.

Notice the use of *energeō* in Ephesians 1:19-20: "According to the working of his mighty power, which he wrought [*energeō*, "energized"] in Christ, when he raised him from the dead." God is so powerful that He raised Christ from the dead.

Whatever God plans He brings to completion. That's the thought behind Paul's series of rhetorical questions in Romans 8:22-35: What shall separate us from the love of Christ?, Who is he that condemneth?, and Who shall lay any thing to the charge of God's elect? The implied answer is "no one." When God plans to do something, it's irrevocable. Ours is a secure hope!

(*c*) Preeminence (v. 12*a*)

"We should be to the praise of his glory."

Here we see salvation from God's perspective. It insures that God receives the glory He deserves. People who don't understand why

God desires praise and glory for Himself don't understand His pure and holy right to it. As sinful creatures we seek glory for the wrong reasons. But we shouldn't project those motives onto God. God seeks glory for the only legitimate reason: He completely deserves it.

So far we have looked at only one side of predestination: God's side. But what about the human side?

(2) From the human perspective (vv. 12b-13a)

"Who first trusted [hoped] in Christ; in whom ye also trusted, after ye heard the word of truth, the gospel of your salvation; in whom also after ye believed."

The human perspective of our divine inheritance is that we had to place our hope in Jesus Christ— we needed to believe. From God's perspective we've been predestinated; from our perspective we had the faith to believe.

(a) The unresolved question

How can predestination and personal faith both exist at the same time? Throughout Scripture there is tension between God's sovereignty and man's will. And it is a tension we are incapable of reconciling completely. But it is our responsibility to believe both truths without reservation, just as they are revealed. We know those truths are in perfect harmony in God's mind, and that should satisfy us.

Someone pictured the divine and human sides of salvation this way: When you look up to heaven you see a sign that reads, "Whosoever will may come." But as soon as you enter heaven and pass by the sign, the back of it reads, "Chosen in Him before the foundation of the world." You need not try to resolve such seemingly irreconcilable truths, just thank and

75

praise God for them. Your responsibility is to respond in faith, knowing that they are harmonized in God's mind.

(b) The ultimate response

Although it is true that the believer is predestinated, he must also respond to the gospel. That's why verse 13 says you hoped in Christ "after listening to the message of truth, the gospel of your salvation—having also believed" (NASB). We must respond in faith and believe.

Romans 10:17 says, "Faith cometh by hearing, and hearing by the word of God." Faith comes by hearing the Word of God. Faith is our response to God's elective purpose. When we believe we confirm God's elective purpose. Believing is our part. We are not required to perform spiritual gymnastics or rituals to be saved. Romans 10:10 says, "With the heart man believeth unto righteousness." The apostle John said, "As many as received him, to them gave he power to become the children of God, even to them that believe on his name" (John 1:12). More than anything else God hates a system of religion that teaches people they can earn their way to heaven.

The Counterfeit Christian Confusion

Many people identify themselves as "born-again" Christians but habitually manifest characteristics that are not Christlike. The result is that they confuse the world about what Christianity really is. A major source of such confusion is the presence of people who claim to be Christians yet believe they'll go to heaven on the basis of their good deeds. A true Christian is not in the process of trying to earn his way into heaven because he knows he cannot. Paul said, "By the deeds of the law there shall no flesh be justified" (Rom. 3:20). The only way to heaven is through faith in Christ. The true Christian believes in Christ for his salvation. His good deeds are the outworkings of his faith, not something done in order to gain salvation (Eph. 2:8-10).

2. The guarantee of our inheritance (vv. 13*b*-14*a*)

"Ye were sealed with that Holy Spirit of promise, who is the earnest of our inheritance until the redemption of the purchased possession."

How do we know that Christ is our inheritance? What is the guarantee that once we jump into Christianity with both feet we won't discover that it's a dead end? The Holy Spirit. God has provided a guarantee because He knows we need to have confidence in our salvation.

We have not yet been totally redeemed. We have been redeemed spiritually, but we await the redemption of our bodies (Rom. 8:23). We haven't received our full inheritance because we're not in heaven. But we know it will happen because we "were sealed with the Holy Spirit of promise, who is the earnest of our inheritance" (Eph. 1:13-14). The Spirit is the guarantee that "the redemption of the purchased possession" will indeed happen.

When we became Christians, God gave each of us the Holy Spirit. Romans 8:9 says, "If any man have not the Spirit of Christ, he is none of his [Christ's]." Paul said, "Your body is the temple of the Holy Spirit" (1 Cor. 6:19). When you became a Christian, God took up residence in your life. That's why you have a new life. The Spirit of God indwells you not only to equip you for ministry but also to guarantee your inheritance. Romans 8:14 says, "As many as are led by the Spirit of God, they are the sons of God." Verse 16 says, "The Spirit himself beareth witness with our spirit, that we are the children of God."

a) The seal (v. 13*b*)

"Ye were sealed with the Holy Spirit of promise."

77

What does it mean to be sealed? In Paul's day an official document would be sealed with wax. An impression would be made in the hot wax with the signet ring of the king or other dignitary. The seal would signify that the document was official.

The Spirit of God is our seal. Let's look at four things that the seal of the Spirit signifies.

(1) A sign of security

In Daniel 6:6-7 prayer was forbidden for thirty days. But Daniel prayed to God anyway and was discovered by the king's men (vv. 10-11). Verse 16 says, "Then the king commanded, and they brought Daniel, and cast him into the den of lions. Now the king spoke and said unto Daniel, Thy God, whom thou servest continually, he will deliver thee." The king didn't want to put Daniel in the lions' den, but he had been persuaded to sign the document by his officials. Verse 17 says, "A stone was brought, and laid upon the mouth of the den; and the king sealed it with his own signet, and with the signet of his lords, that the purpose might not be changed concerning Daniel." Anyone who saw the king's seal knew he dare not open the lions' den because the highest authority in the land had sealed it.

When Christ was buried in a tomb, the Roman guard rolled a stone across the opening and then sealed it with the seal of Rome (Matt. 27:66). That meant no one was to open the seal unless it was a power greater than Rome. And a power greater than Rome did break the seal—the power of God!

When you became a Christian, God put His Holy Spirit in you. He stamped us with His signet ring, thus declaring us secure. No one can ever touch our lives unless he is a higher authority than Almighty God—and there is no such authority.

(2) A sign of authenticity

When God gave us His Holy Spirit, He declared us to be authentic children of the King. The only authentic Christian is one who possesses the Holy Spirit.

(3) A sign of a completed transaction

Jeremiah was a faithful prophet who did what God asked. One of the things God asked him to do was buy a piece of property (Jer. 32:7). After Jeremiah bought the field, he sealed the transaction (v. 14). Similarly, when you put your faith in Jesus Christ, God gave you the Holy Spirit to complete the transaction.

(4) A sign of authority

When God gave us the Holy Spirit, we were enabled to speak from God's Word with authority (cf. John 16:23).

When God gave you the Holy Spirit, He gave you the only guarantee you'll ever need.

b) The guarantee (v. 14a)

"[The Holy Spirit] is the earnest of our inheritance until the redemption of the purchased possession."

The Greek word translated "earnest" (*arrabōn*) means "down payment." Just so we know that the promises God has given us are legitimate, God gives us the Holy Spirit as a down payment on those promises. That's how we know He won't renege on the rest of His promises.

A form of *arrabōn* also came to be used for an engagement ring. The Bible tells us that one day there will be a marriage supper where Christ is the Bridegroom and the church is the bride (Rev. 19:7-10). We know the wedding will take place because He gave the church an engagement ring—a symbol of commitment. The Holy Spirit is that engagement ring. He represents God's commitment and investment in us. So that we'll know His inheritance is laid up for us, He has given us a down payment: the Spirit of promise. The Spirit continually reminds us that we are children of God and will one day see the fulfillment of God's promises.

3. The goal of our inheritance (v. 14*b*)

"Unto the praise of his glory."

God wants to be glorified through you. He didn't make you a Christian for your own glory. The moment you seek to exalt yourself as an authority is the moment you enter competition with the eternal God. That kind of competition can have only one winner, and it won't be you! We're to be God's servants.

I am humbled by God's grace in my life. What He has done for me is to the praise of His glory. My only desire is to lift up Jesus Christ. My heart is filled with praise for One who would be so gracious to such a sinner as myself. I hope it is your desire to be to the praise of His glory.

Focusing on the Facts

1. Why are the promises of God more believable than the promises of men? Support your answer with Scripture (see pp. 68-69).
2. What are two possible translations of Ephesians 1:11? Explain each one (see pp. 69-70).
3. What is our inheritance? Is it strictly future? Explain (see p. 71).
4. What is the ground of the believer's inheritance (see p. 72)?
5. What major truth did Paul teach in Romans 6:3-5? What are some of the results of that truth (see pp. 72-73)?

6. From the divine perspective, how did we obtain our heavenly inheritance (see p. 73)?
7. How is God's power connected to His predetermined plans (see p. 74)?
8. According to Ephesians 1:19-20, what did God's power do (see p. 74)?
9. Why is salvation presented from God's perspective (Eph. 1:12; see pp. 74-75)?
10. From the human perspective, how did we obtain our divine inheritance (see p. 75)?
11. How can we resolve the conflict between the human and divine perspectives on salvation (see pp. 75-76)?
12. If we are predestined, must we respond to the gospel? Why (see p. 76)?
13. What is our guarantee that we will receive our inheritance (Eph. 1:13-14; see p. 77)?
14. What is significant about being sealed with the Holy Spirit? How do each of the four characteristics of a seal apply to a Christian (see pp. 78-79)?
15. What does the Greek word translated "earnest" mean (see p. 79)?
16. What is the goal of our inheritance (see p. 80)?

Pondering the Principles

1. How many of the promises of God are ours (2 Cor. 1:20)? Why is it important to know what God has promised us? Write down as many of the promises you can remember that God has given us. Keep that list, and as you read your Bible for devotions or study, record additional promises you come across. Whenever you feel sad, pull out your list as an encouragement and thank God for what He has promised to give you.

2. Reread the section on the goal of our inheritance (see p. 80), and ask yourself this question: Do you exalt yourself over God? You may not do so in an overt way, but it is easy to forget God as you make your plans for the day. Seek to live each moment for God—to involve Him in everything you do each day. Every moment you do that it will be "unto the praise of his glory."

6
Our Resources in Christ—Part 1

Outline

Introduction
A. The Power to Understand God's Truth
B. The Prayer to Understand God's Truth
C. The Priority of Understanding God's Truth
  1. Knowing our position
    a) Defining the parameters
      (1) In our secular lives
      (2) In our spiritual lives
        (*a*) Improper motivation
        (*b*) Internal motivation
    b) Distinguishing the parameters
  2. Keeping our perspective
    a) A problematic concept
    b) A positional completeness
      (1) Colossians 2:10
      (2) Hebrews 10:14
      (3) 2 Peter 1:3-7

Lesson
I. Thanksgiving (vv. 15-16)
A. The Source of His Thanksgiving
B. The Specifics of His Thanksgiving
  1. Faith in the Lord Jesus
    a) Philippians 2:10-11
    b) Romans 10:9
  2. Love for all the saints
    a) Philippians 2:2
    b) 1 John 3:17-18

II. Supplication (vv. 17-23)
  A. The Spirit of Paul's Request (v. 17)
    1. The believer's unnecessary search
      a) Illustrated
      b) Identified
    2. The believer's necessary attitude
      a) Its source
      b) Its significance
        (1) Incorrect interpretations
        (2) The correct interpretation

Conclusion

Introduction

Ephesians 1:15-23 is a prayer of the apostle Paul in response to the theological treatise of verses 3-14. Paul told believers what they possess in Jesus Christ. He discussed the believer's election, redemption, and inheritance.

A. The Power to Understand God's Truth

The truths of verses 3-14 are beyond the full grasp of the human mind. We can't reach that deep into the truth of God. First Corinthians 2 tells us why. Verse 9 says, "Eye hath not seen, nor ear heard, neither have entered into the heart of man, the things which God hath prepared for them that love him." Man is unable to understand God's truth both externally and internally. In verses 10-11 Paul identifies the only way man can know God's truth: "God hath revealed them unto us by his Spirit; for the Spirit searcheth all things, yea, the deep things of God. For what man knoweth the things of a man, except the spirit of a man which is in him? Even so the things of God knoweth no man, but the Spirit of God." We must depend on the Holy Spirit to understand the deep things of God. That is the only way we can understand Ephesians 1:3-14, which contains some of the deepest truths we can ever know.

B. The Prayer to Understand God's Truth

Having delineated what a believer has in Christ, Paul then prays for believers to understand those truths. In Ephesians 1 Paul begins his epistle by describing our position in Christ and then praying that we would understand it. In chapter 2 he describes our position in Christ and in chapter 3 again prays that we would understand what he said. Then beginning in chapter 4 he tells us how to respond to our position. The point is that you cannot live out what you do not understand—you can't function on principles you don't know. Unfortunately many Christians today are frustrated because they're trying to live a life that's never been clearly defined for them.

Paul knew he couldn't merely pass information on to people, so he prayed for God to make it real to them. That's why the apostles said, "We will give ourselves continually to prayer, and to the ministry of the word" (Acts 6:4). Why? Because the ministry of the Word must be energized by the Spirit of God. And God's men seek that through intercessory prayer on behalf of God's people. The central focus of such prayer is not for the physical ailments of the people but that they would receive "the spirit of wisdom and revelation in the knowledge of him, the eyes of [their] understanding being enlightened; that [they] may know what is the hope of his calling" (Eph. 1:17-18). It's not enough just to teach; God's men must pray that their teaching be energized by the Spirit of God in the hearts of the people.

C. The Priority of Understanding God's Truth

1. Knowing our position

   a) Defining the parameters

      (1) In our secular lives

          Knowing your position is important. When people are hired for a new job, they usually receive a job description. Whether you're an executive or a worker on an assembly line, you still need to know your role. The same thing is true in athletics. Coaches stress the importance of knowing your position so that you can play it properly.

(2) In our spiritual lives

In any assignment we're given, the parameters usually are defined before you're asked to fulfill the assignment. After the parameters are defined, you must understand them before you can perform the task. The same thing is true in the Christian life: People won't behave in the desired manner unless they understand the definition and parameters of what they've been asked to do. Unfortunately, in many churches pastors tell the congregation what to do but never help them understand why they should do it.

(a) Improper motivation

Pastors are supposed to exhort people to live the Christian life, to do what's right, and to dedicate themselves to God. Unfortunately, some pastors use pep talks, guilt, intimidation, and peer pressure as a way of exhorting their people. Each of those motives for action bypasses the true motive for living the Christian life.

(b) Internal motivation

The basis of understanding who you are in Christ is simply knowing your position. That understanding alone is the foundation upon which you are to operate. If all you do is challenge yourself to live the Christian life and beat yourself into conformity, you will never understand your position.

Paul prayed that the people would understand that they are one with the eternal God through Christ and that all the blessings of heaven are theirs. Then he prayed they would act accordingly. Christians need to be taught positional truth so that they will know how to act. If they don't know who they are, they won't know why they should act a certain way.

b) Distinguishing the parameters

In studying the Bible, a distinction must be made between position and practice. If you don't understand which statements are positional and which are practical, you'll never interpret the Bible correctly. For example, in 1 Corinthians 3:17 Paul tells the Corinthians they are holy. But he also said to them, "Let us cleanse ourselves from all filthiness" (2 Cor. 7:1). On the surface you might think the Corinthians were holy some of the time and filthy the rest of the time. The fact is that they were holy before God in Christ in their position but not in their practice. Positionally a believer is perfectly holy and righteous in Christ. That is an eternal, unchanging reality. But his practice is weighed down by any unholy and unrighteous behavior. The goal of the Christian life is to make your practice equal your position.

2. Keeping our perspective

Christian growth has nothing to do with your position in Christ. When you were saved and placed in Christ, His righteousness was imputed to you. All your sins were forgiven, you received eternal life, and you were made perfect. That is your position before God. Your growth takes place through your practice, not your position.

a) A problematic concept

Many Christians think God likes them better as they grow and mature. But God isn't like a parent who tells his child he won't love him if he misbehaves—or that he will love him more if he behaves. What you do or don't do has no effect on your position before God. You can't do anything to make God like you more or less. He loves you perfectly in Christ.

87

b) A positional completeness

Ephesians 1:6 tells us we are "accepted in the Beloved." We already possess God's favor and grace because we are one with Christ. God sees us just as He sees Jesus Christ. Positionally our standing is perfect.

(1) Colossians 2:10—"Ye are complete in him."

(2) Hebrews 10:14—"By one offering [Christ] hath perfected forever them that are sanctified."

(3) 2 Peter 1:3-7—"According as his divine power hath given unto us all things that pertain unto life and godliness, through the knowledge of him that hath called us to glory and virtue; by which are given unto us exceedingly great and precious promises, that by these ye might be partakers of the divine nature, having escaped the corruption that is in the world through lust. And beside this, giving all diligence, add to your faith virtue; and to virtue, knowledge; and to knowledge, self-control, and to self-control, patience; and to patience, godliness; and to godliness, brotherly kindness; and to brotherly kindness, love."

Are You a Spiritual Polliwog?

The Christian life is the process of becoming what you already are in Christ. Consider the difference between the development of a polliwog and a child. A polliwog is born as a shapeless mass with a tail. After a while it sprouts some legs. Eventually it takes the form of a frog or a toad. However, when a human baby is born into the world it comes with all the necessary parts—they merely need to grow. The same thing is true of a Christian. When you were born into the family of God, you were not a spiritual polliwog. You were complete. You have all the parts of a mature Christian; you simply need to grow.

Solomon was right when he said, "I know that, whatsoever God doeth, it shall be forever; nothing can be put to it, nor any thing taken from it" (Eccles. 3:14). When God saves a person, that work

88

is total and complete. He stands perfect before God. The rest of his life is just a matter of growing so that his practice will match his position.

Instead of seeking more favor with God or trying to be more fit for heaven, we should thank God, who has "made us fit to be partakers of the inheritance of the saints in light" (Col. 1:12). We already are fit for heaven. Nothing we do will make God like us more than He already does.

When we understand all that Ephesians 1:3-14 says we have in Christ, that ought to change the way we live. People cannot be exhorted to live righteously unless they understand who they are. That's why Paul offers up a prayer in Ephesians 1:15-23. Constant exhortation without an understanding of basic theology brings people under guilt. And that certainly won't motivate them. But the mature Christian understands his privileges, possessions, and resources so he can live consistently with who he is.

Theology: The Basis of Our Practice

In Ephesians 4:1 Paul says, "I therefore, the prisoner of the Lord, beseech you that ye walk worthy of the vocation to which ye are called." Paul devoted the first three chapters of Ephesians to describe God's calling; he devoted the last three to clarifying how believers should live. Similarly, in the book of Romans he devotes eleven chapters to theology before telling the believers how to live. Galatians has four chapters on theology and two on practice. Colossians 1:1–2:5 is theological; the remainder is practical. We have to build our practice on our position.

Lesson

I. THANKSGIVING (vv. 15-16)

"Wherefore, I also, after I heard of your faith in the Lord Jesus, and love unto all the saints, cease not to give thanks for you, making mention of you in my prayers."

"Wherefore" takes us back to Paul's previous statements (vv. 3-14). Paul's prayer is based on the believer's tremendous inheritance in Christ.

A. The Source of His Thanksgiving

How did Paul hear about the Ephesian church's faith and love? Some four years had passed since he last ministered in Ephesus. He was now in prison (Eph. 3:1; 4:1; 6:20), probably his first Roman imprisonment. But he also enjoyed some liberties during his imprisonment. For example, people were allowed to visit him (Acts 28:30). No doubt several Christians brought reports of all the churches in Asia Minor. Sea travel was common in those days.

B. The Specifics of His Thanksgiving

Paul heard two things about the Ephesians: their "faith in the Lord Jesus, and love unto all the saints." Faith and love are the basic indicators of a true Christian. A believer's faith in Christ is proven by his love toward all saints. First John 2:9-11 says that if you claim to have saving faith yet hate your brother, you're a liar. Jesus said, "By this shall all men know that ye are my disciples, if ye have love one to another" (John 13:35). Love is defined as self-sacrificing service of one to another. True faith will result in love.

1. Faith in the Lord Jesus

Salvation begins with faith—with believing that Jesus is Lord. Scripture is clear on that issue. Some people claim that Jesus can be received as Savior and then later as Lord. But the Bible doesn't teach that. Jesus must be acknowledged as Lord because He *is* Lord.

a) Philippians 2:10-11—"At the name of Jesus every knee should bow, of things in heaven, and things in earth, and things under the earth, and that every tongue should confess that Jesus Christ is Lord, to the glory of God, the Father."

b) Romans 10:9—"If you confess with your mouth Jesus as Lord, and believe in your heart that God raised Him from the dead, you shall be saved" (NASB).

Paul knew the Ephesians' faith was genuine because it was placed in the Lord Jesus. He is not received as Savior and then later as Lord. He must be received as Lord—if He is to be received at all—because that's who He is.

2. Love for all the saints

Notice that their love was indiscriminate. A true Christian doesn't pick and choose the objects of his love; whoever comes into his life is to be loved.

Sometimes we hear Christians say, "I love him in the Lord," which seems to imply they have no personal affection for or commitment to the needs of the individual. They extend a spiritualized love only because the other person is a believer and they feel like they have to. But that is not Christlike love. To love someone in the Lord is to love him as Jesus loves him—genuinely and sacrificially. The world picks and chooses, but a Christian is to show "love unto *all* the saints" (Eph. 1:15, emphasis added). We must not discriminate.

a) Philippians 2:2—Paul said, "Fulfill ye my joy, that ye be like-minded, having the same love." We are to love everyone the same.

b) 1 John 3:17-18—"Whosoever hath this world's good, and seeth his brother have need, and shutteth up his compassions from him, how dwelleth the love of God in him? My little children, let us not love in word, neither in tongue, but in deed and in truth."

You can learn all the theology you want, but if you don't love, you're nothing but "sounding bronze, or a tinkling cymbal" (1 Cor. 13:1). True salvation goes from the head and heart of the believer to other believers and to an unbelieving world in Christ's name.

The Balance of Faith and Love

The Ephesian church had a good beginning, but the resurrected Lord had this to say about it many years later: "I have somewhat against thee, because thou hast left thy first love" (Rev. 2:4). The Ephesian church went out of existence not much later. Faith and love must be kept in balance.

- Monks and hermits had a loyalty to Christ that separated them from the world. They lived alone to contemplate their faith, but it was loveless faith that rarely touched anyone.

- The heresy hunters of the Spanish Inquisition had loyalty to a faith that caused them to persecute anyone who was different. Theirs was a loveless faith.

- The Pharisees of Jesus' day had a loyalty to God that made them hateful of others, but theirs was a loveless faith.

Many so-called Christians in churches today are hateful, bitter, and resentful of other Christians. That reveals a loveless faith—a faith that might not be genuine, saving faith.

Genuine faith is marked by love for all the saints. You can't love Christ and put your faith in Him without loving the people He loves. First John 5:1-2 says, "Whosoever believeth that Jesus is the Christ is born of God; and everyone that loveth him that begot loveth him also that is begotten of him."

II. SUPPLICATION (vv. 17-23)

A. The Spirit of Paul's Request (v. 17)

"[I pray] that the God of our Lord Jesus Christ, the Father of glory, may give unto you the spirit of wisdom and revelation in the knowledge of him."

1. The believer's unnecessary search

   a) Illustrated

   In his commentary on Ephesians, Warren Wiersbe tells an interesting story about William Randolph Hearst, the late newspaper publisher (*Be Rich* [Wheaton, Ill.: Victor, 1976], pp. 29-30). Hearst was known to have invested a fortune in collecting great works of art. As he collected them he stored them in various warehouses. One day he read about an incredibly valuable piece of art. Determined to purchase it for himself, he sent his agent to look for it. Months went by before the agent returned and reported to Hearst that he found it. When Hearst asked him where, the agent told him it was in one of his own warehouses; he had purchased it years before! That's quite an illustration of someone's searching for something he already has.

   b) Identified

   In Ephesians 1:17 Paul prays that the Lord might spare Christians from a frantic search for things they already possess. He asks God to give them "the spirit of wisdom and revelation in the knowledge of him" so that they might know what they possess and make use of it.

   The typical Christian wastes time asking God for things He has already given. We ask God for strength, yet the Bible says we can do all things through Christ who strengthens us (Phil. 4:13). We ask for love, yet the Bible says, "The love of God is shed abroad in our hearts" (Rom. 5:5). We pray for grace, yet God says, "My grace is sufficient for thee" (2 Cor. 12:9). And we pray for peace, but the Bible says, "The peace of God, which passeth all understanding, shall keep your hearts and minds through Christ Jesus" (Phil. 4:7). We need to know what we have in Christ, and the wisdom to apply it.

Our minds cannot conceive of the riches of our position in Christ. Only the Spirit can search the deep things of God and reveal them to us.

2. The believer's necessary attitude

a) Its source

Knowing that we can't understand God's truth on our own, Paul called on "the God of our Lord Jesus Christ, the Father of glory" (Eph. 1:17). That is a designation of God linking the Father to the Son in terms of essential nature. The One to whom all glory belongs is the same in essence as the Lord Jesus Christ.

b) Its significance

Paul prayed that God might "give unto [us] the spirit of wisdom and revelation in the knowledge of him." The Greek word translated "the spirit" is an anarthrous construction—it appears without an article. So Paul was praying that God would give us a spirit of wisdom and revelation.

(1) Incorrect interpretations

Some people believe Paul was asking God to grant believers the Holy Spirit. But we don't need to ask for the Holy Spirit because God already gave Him to us (1 Cor. 12:13). First Corinthians 6:19 says that our bodies are temples of the Holy Spirit, and Romans 8:9 says that all Christians possess the Holy Spirit. Others say Paul was referring to the human spirit, but we have had a spirit and soul all our lives.

(2) The correct interpretation

The Greek word translated "spirit" is *pneuma*, from which we derive the English words *pneumatic*

94

and *pneumonia*. *Pneuma* can be translated "wind," "breath," "air," or "spirit." But it can also refer to a disposition or an attitude that governs one's soul. For example, in the Sermon on the Mount Jesus said, "Blessed are the poor in spirit" (Matt. 5:3). He wasn't referring to the Holy Spirit or the human spirit, He was referring to an attitude of humility. When we see someone who is sad we might say he has a sad spirit. When we see someone vigorously play some sport, we say he is spirited. Or when we see someone who is happy we say he is in high spirits. All those examples are attitudes. I believe that's what Paul was referring to in Ephesians 1:17. He wanted God to give believers an attitude of wisdom and revelation about Christ.

However, I do believe that the Holy Spirit and the human spirit are implied in verse 17. Paul's prayer was essentially, "May the Holy Spirit work on your spirit to create an attitude of wisdom and revelation about Christ." We know the Holy Spirit must be involved because only He can search the deep things of God (1 Cor. 2:10).

The Greek word translated "revelation," used in verse 17 as a synonym of wisdom, refers to God's imparting of knowledge to us, while "wisdom" could emphasize our use of that knowledge. We must know about our position and resources in Christ before we can effectively use them. Paul wanted the Ephesians to have a full, deep knowledge of Christ, not just an intellectual acquaintance with the basic facts.

Conclusion

The Christian life is predicated on what you know. Truth must be revealed to you before you can practice it. That's why I devote so much of my time to teaching God's Word. Paul prayed that we would gain a divine perspective—that we would set our "affection on things above, not on things on the earth" (Col. 3:2).

Focusing on the Facts

1. What is the only way a person will ever understand the deep things of God (1 Cor. 2:9-11; see p. 84)?
2. In Ephesians 1-3 Paul's pattern is to describe our position in Christ and then pray that we might understand it. Why? What does he begin to do in chapter 4 (see p. 85)?
3. What must a believer know before he understands who he is in Christ (see pp. 85-86)?
4. What is the difference between our position and our practice? Why is being aware of that distinction necessary when we study the Bible (see p. 87)?
5. Why did Paul tell the Corinthians to cleanse themselves from all filthiness when he already had declared them holy (see p. 87)?
6. What is wrong with the perspective that God loves us more when we grow in spiritual maturity (see p. 87)?
7. Which is the better analogy to use in describing a Christian: a polliwog or a human baby? Why (see p. 88)?
8. How do people usually respond when they are constantly exhorted without being taught basic theology (see p. 89)?
9. What two things did Paul hear about the Ephesian church that caused him to give thanks (see p. 90)?
10. According to 1 John 2:9-11, what conclusion can you make about someone who claims to have saving faith but hates his brother (see p. 90)?
11. True faith will result in _____ (see p. 90)?
12. What is wrong with the idea that Jesus can be received as Savior but not as Lord (see pp. 90-91)?
13. What quality of love is evidenced by the phrase "love unto all the saints" (Eph. 1:15; see p. 91)?
14. In what unnecessary search do most believers participate (see p. 93)?
15. "Spirit" in Ephesians 1:17 refers to what? Why (see pp. 94-95)?
16. Define "revelation" and "wisdom" as used by Paul in Ephesians 1:17 (see p. 95).

Pondering the Principles

1. To interpret the Bible correctly we must be able to differentiate which statements discuss our position and which ones deal with our practice. Look up the following pairs of verses and determine which passage is positional and which one is practical: Romans 5:1 and 14:19, Romans 8:9 and Ephesians 4:30, Ephesians 1:5 and 5:1, and 1 John 2:15 and 5:4-5.

2. Do you have trouble loving someone in your church, your Bible study, or your family? Read 1 Corinthians 13:4-8, and list each characteristic of true love. Which ones give you the most trouble? Why? Ask the Lord to help you exhibit each quality of true love toward that individual you are struggling to love. Thank God for His Holy Spirit, who will strengthen you to carry out His will in your life.

7
Our Resources in Christ—Part 2
Is There Something More?

Outline

Introduction
A. The Search for More
B. The Substance of Salvation
C. The Sufficiency of Christ
   1. The purpose of the Colossian epistle
   2. The additions of the Colossian errorists
      a) Christ plus philosophy (Col. 2:8)
      b) Christ plus legalism (Col. 2:16-17)
      c) Christ plus mysticism (Col. 2:18)
      d) Christ plus asceticism (Col. 2:20-23)
   3. The point of the Colossian example

Review
I. Thanksgiving (vv. 15-16)
II. Supplication (vv. 17-23)
  A. The Spirit of Paul's Request (v. 17)

Lesson
B. The Specifics of Paul's Request (vv. 18-23)
   1. The greatness of God's plan (v. 18)
      a) The organ of spiritual perception (v. 18*a*)
        (1) The heart examined
          (*a*) The seat of the emotions
            i) Song of Solomon 5:4
            ii) Psalm 22:14
            iii) Lamentations 2:11
            iv) 1 John 3:17

Introduction

A. The Search for More

There is a trend in Christianity today that deeply troubles me. It is the quest for something more—the idea that being in Christ is not sufficient. People talk of getting more of Christ, more of the Holy Spirit, and more of His power. They view the resources of Christ as a pharmaceutical prescription, doled out one dose at a time. Others think you must qualify to receive them by a particular ritual. I talked to a woman who said she searched for everything she could because she wanted to "get all of Jesus." The implication of that thinking is that people don't get all of Jesus when they are saved. That would be like obtaining the right to His resources but not receiving any of it in their hearts and minds. Do we need more of God, more of Jesus, and more of the Holy Spirit—or do we receive everything in salvation?

B. The Substance of Salvation

Second Peter 1:3 answers that question: "According as his divine power hath given unto us *all things* that pertain unto life and godliness, through the knowledge of him" (emphasis added). The biblical view of the doctrine of salvation is that salvation grants the believer everything in Christ. There is no need to search for something more. Such a search undermines the essence of salvation. It contradicts what Jesus said just before He died: *Tetelestai*, which is best translated, "It is completed," "it is finished," or "it is fulfilled." To seek for something more indicates a belief that something is missing in salvation.

C. The Sufficiency of Christ

A good illustration of this particular conflict is to look at the problem the Colossian church was facing.

1. The purpose of the Colossian epistle

Like so many of the early churches in the Roman world, the Colossian church was exposed to many kinds of heresies. One of the most prevalent, which could be traced back to the Essenes, claimed that Christ was not enough for a person to be saved—that something more needed to be added. That heresy is quite similar to what we are seeing today.

The apostle Paul wrote the Colossians to remind them that Jesus Christ is absolutely, totally, and completely sufficient. In chapter 1 he says that God "hath delivered us from the power of darkness and hath translated us into the kingdom of his dear Son; in whom we have redemption through his blood, even the forgiveness of sins; who is the image of the invisible God, the first-born of all creation; for by him were all things created, that are in heaven, and that are in earth, visible and invisible, whether they be thrones, or dominions, or principalities, or powers—all things were created by him, and for him; and he is before all things, and by him all things consist. And he is the head of the body, the church; who is the beginning, the first-born from the dead, that in all things he might have the preeminence. For it pleased the Father that in him should all fullness dwell" (vv. 13-19). Paul is saying that Christ is everything, and that is also his message in Ephesians 1.

2. The additions of the Colossian errorists

The Colossian church was exposed to people advocating that a person needed Christ plus other things to be elevated to the true spiritual plane.

a) Christ plus philosophy (Col. 2:8)

The Colossian errorists added vain human wisdom to the reality of Christ. That is similar to what we know today as liberalism, neoorthodoxy, or modernism. Paul warned the Colossians of that error, saying, "Beware lest any man spoil you through philosophy and vain deceit, after the tradition of men, after the rudiments of the world [the rudiments of human religion, which is philosophical rather than theological], and not after Christ" (v. 8). Christ is sufficient; such philosophy is not.

b) Christ plus legalism (Col. 2:16-17)

Paul said, "Let no man, therefore, judge you in food, or in drink, or in respect of a feast day, or of the new moon, or of a sabbath day" (v. 16). He was telling the Colossians not to allow anyone to evaluate their spirituality on the basis of keeping religious rituals. In verse 17 he says why: They "are a shadow of things to come; but the body [substance] is Christ."

c) Christ plus mysticism (Col. 2:18)

Paul said, "Do not let anyone who delights in false humility and the worship of angels disqualify you for the prize. Such a person goes into great detail about what he has seen, and his unspiritual mind puffs him up with idle notions" (v. 18, NIV). People today believe that Christ is not enough—that some heavenly vision or spellbinding experience is necessary for salvation to be real. But according to verse 18 those things result in false humility and pride.

d) Christ plus asceticism (Col. 2:20-23)

Asceticism is a monastic life—a life of self-denial. Paul said, "If ye be dead with Christ from the rudiments of the world, why, as though living in the world, are ye subject to ordinances (touch not; taste not; handle not; which all are to perish with the using) after the commandments and doctrines of men? These things have indeed a show of wisdom in will-worship, and humility, and neglecting of the body, not in any honor to the satisfying of the flesh" (vv. 20-23). Ascetics practiced self-flagellation and anything else that deprived their bodies, but all to no avail in God's sight.

3. The point of the Colossian example

There always have been (and always will be) people who claim that Jesus Christ is not enough—that something must be added to His saving work. Paul's answer to that is summed up in Colossians 2:9-10: "In him [Christ] dwelleth all the fullness of the Godhead bodily. And ye are complete in him." Nothing is missing in Christ. In verse 12 Paul says you have been "buried with him in baptism, in which also ye are risen with him through the faith of the operation of God, who hath raised him from the dead." We have no reason to search for something more. We need to use the resources Christ already gave us.

In Ephesians 1:3-14 Paul carefully outlines the believer's resources and position in Christ. He told us who we are and what we possess—a magnificent statement of what Christ accomplished in our salvation. Verse 3 makes clear that nothing is missing: "Blessed be the God and Father of our Lord Jesus Christ, who hath blessed us with *all* spiritual blessings" (emphasis added).

The great truths of the believer's position in Christ are so profound and difficult for the human mind to grasp that Paul prayed for his readers to understand the reality of what he said. A man of God gives himself to the study of the Word and prayer (Acts 6:4). He studies the Word to teach its truths and prays that God will enable the people to understand it. For that the human mind requires a special work by the Spirit of God. First John 2:27 says that God has given us an anointing of the Spirit of God, who teaches us all things.

I. THANKSGIVING (vv. 15-16; see pp. 89-92)

"I also, after I heard of your faith in the Lord Jesus, and love unto all the saints, cease not to give thanks for you, making mention of you in my prayers."

II. SUPPLICATION (vv. 17-23)

A. The Spirit of Paul's Request (v. 17; see pp. 92-95)

"That the God of our Lord Jesus Christ, the Father of glory, may give unto you the spirit of wisdom and revelation in the knowledge of Him."

Going Beyond Human Comprehension

In 1 Corinthians 2:9-12 Paul says, "As it is written, Eye hath not seen, nor ear heard, neither have entered into the heart of man, the things which God hath prepared for them that love him. But God hath revealed them unto us by his Spirit; for the Spirit searcheth all things, yea, the deep things of God. For what man knoweth the things of a man, except the spirit of a man which is in him? Even so the things of God knoweth no man, but the Spirit of God. Now we have received not the spirit of the world, but the Spirit who is of God; that we might know the things that are freely given to us of God." God has given us the ability to conceive of what is beyond human senses to hear, touch, or see.

Some claim that when you become a Christian you don't receive the Holy Spirit. But if that were true, you would never understand the supernatural principles that govern the Christian life. That's why Paul said, "If any man have not the Spirit of Christ, he is none of his" (Rom. 8:9). All Christians possess the Spirit. He is our resident truth teacher. He allows us to comprehend what is beyond human comprehension.

Lesson

B. The Specifics of Paul's Request (vv. 18-23)

Paul had three truths he wanted us to understand: the greatness of God's plan, the greatness of God's power, and the greatness of God's person.

1. The greatness of God's plan (v. 18)

"The eyes of your understanding being enlightened; that ye may know what is the hope of his calling, and what the riches of the glory of his inheritance in the saints."

The "calling" occurred before the world began, and the "hope" is in what awaits us. Paul prayed that we would understand who we are and what God has prepared for us.

a) The organ of spiritual perception (v. 18a)

"The eyes of your understanding being enlightened."

The Greek word translated "understanding" is *kardias*, from which we derive the English word *cardiac*. It means "heart." The Greek text literally says, "The eyes of your heart being enlightened."

In verses 15-17 we discovered that God is the source of spiritual enlightenment and that the Holy Spirit is the channel. The object of that enlightenment is knowledge of Christ (v. 17). In verse 18 Paul identifies the heart as the organ of spiritual understanding.

(1) The heart examined

Many people misunderstand the meaning of *heart* in Scripture because our American culture has so often designated the heart to refer to the emotions. Many of our love songs refer to the heart. But ancient peoples, including the Jewish race, did not see the heart as the seat of their emotions.

(*a*) The seat of the emotions

When the Jewish people spoke about their emotions, they didn't refer to the heart, but to the gut or visceral area—translated "bowels" in archaic English Bibles (Heb., *meim*; Gk., *splanchna*). The Jewish person naturally associated his feelings with with his stomach because that's where he felt his emotions. Today we'll say we have a "gut feeling." When you become nervous or anxious you feel those emotions in your stomach.

Let's look at some examples.

i) Song of Solomon 5:4—The bride said, "My beloved put in his hand by the hold of the door, and my bowels were moved for him" (KJV). She had a feeling of anticipation and excitement in her stomach.

ii) Psalm 22:14—In a prophetic look at Christ's crucifixion, David wrote, "I am poured out like water, and all my bones are out of joint: my heart is like wax; it is melted in the midst of my bowels" (KJV).

iii) Lamentations 2:11—When Jeremiah cried over the destruction of his people he said,

106

"Mine eyes do fail with tears, my bowels are troubled, my liver is poured upon the earth" (KJV).

iv) 1 John 3:17—"Whoso hath this world's good, and seeth his brother have need, and shutteth up his bowels of compassion from him, how dwelleth the love of God in him?" (KJV).

(b) The seat of understanding

The Jewish person didn't think of the heart as referring to feelings, but to thinking. That's why Paul chose the Greek word *kardias*, which can be translated either "heart" or "understanding."

i) Proverbs 23:7—"As [a man] thinketh in his heart, so is he."

ii) Matthew 12:34—"Out of the abundance of the heart the mouth speaketh."

iii) Jeremiah 17:9—"The heart is deceitful above all things, and desperately wicked; who can know it?"

The heart in that context refers to the thinking processes—the mind, will, and understanding.

The organ of spiritual perception for the believer is our thinking processes, not the emotions. God doesn't appeal to our emotions; He appeals to our minds and will.

Do Your Emotions Obstruct the Truth?

Christianity is not designed to appeal to the emotions; emotions are designed to respond to the mind. Anything under the guise of Christianity that attempts to appeal to the emotions and bypass the mind will generate a response that has nothing to do with truth.

In 2 Corinthians 6:11 Paul says, "O ye Corinthians, our speech to you is candid, our heart [Gk., *kardias*] is wide open." Paul had an open mind toward the Corinthians—he was prepared to communicate all he knew about God to them. But in verse 13 he says, "In fair exchange (I speak as unto my children), open wide your hearts [minds] to us." Paul wanted to teach them, but he needed their cooperation. This was the problem: "On our part there is no constraint, but there is constraint in your affections [Gk., *splanchna*, "guts," "emotions"]" (v. 12). Their emotions prevented Paul from communicating God's truth to them. The Greek text says that they were tightened in their guts. Today we would say they were emotionally uptight. Paul was saying that the work of God in the lives of the Corinthians was hindered because their emotions got in the way of the truth. So be warned: Whenever you put your feelings before God's truth, you will short-circuit the truth, and your emotions will run your life.

(2) The heart enlightened

When Paul prayed that the Ephesians' hearts might be enlightened, he was asking for them to have an understanding of God's plan. The Holy Spirit enriches the believer's mind with an understanding of divine truth and then relates it to his life.

(a) The principle

Paul told the Colossians that they didn't need vain human wisdom, legalism, asceticism, or mysticism (Col. 2:8-23). But they did need to "let the word of Christ dwell in [them] richly" (3:16). And it is the Holy Spirit who drives Scripture into a person's mind.

(b) The practice

After His resurrection, Jesus appeared to two disciples traveling on the road to Emmaus, but they didn't recognize Him (Luke 24:13-16). They walked along for several miles as Jesus taught them about Himself from Scripture. Later, as they were eating with Him, "their eyes were opened, and they recognized him; and he vanished out of their sight. And they said one to another, Did not our heart [mind] burn within us, while he talked with us along the way, and while he opened to us the scriptures?" (vv. 31-32). Knowing Scripture won't make your heart burn until Christ, through His Spirit, drives it deep into your mind.

b) The ordination of a special plan (v. 18*b*)

"That ye may know what is the hope of his calling, and . . . the riches of the glory of his inheritance in the saints."

(1) A great plan

Paul wanted the Ephesian believers to understand what God had planned for them. He wanted them to know about their election, redemption, and inheritance. That plan was not an afterthought, but the master plan of the eternal God. Believers were a part of God's plan even before the world began. Paul realized that once believers understood all that their salvation entailed, they would act accordingly.

When I dwell on that plan, I realize that some day all we who love Christ will be like Him (1 John 3:2). How incredible to realize that we are joint-heirs with Christ (Rom. 8:17)!

(2) A rich plan

Verse 18 tells us what's involved in God's great plan: "The riches of the glory of his inheritance in the saints." We are saints (Gk., *hagios*, "holy ones"). We were made holy in Jesus Christ. We are God's children and will receive an inheritance. But notice that it isn't merely an inheritance—it's "the riches of the glory of his inheritance." That means words can't describe the greatness of the inheritance God has planned for us.

2. The greatness of God's power (vv. 19-20)

   a) His power identified (v. 19)

   "What is the exceeding greatness of his power toward us who believe, according to the working of his mighty power."

   Paul was trying to describe how powerful we are, so he used every word for power he could imagine. There are four different Greek words used for power in verse 19.

   (1) Defined

       (*a*) *Dunamis*—"The exceeding greatness of his power [*dunamis*]." We derive the English word *dynamite* from *dunamis*. It refers to inherent power.

       (*b*) *Energeia*—"According to the working [*energeia*]." That word is the basis for the English word *energy*. It refers to operative power.

       (*c*) *Kratos*—"The working of his mighty [*kratos*]." Sometimes *kratos* is translated "dominion." It refers to ultimate power.

       (*d*) *Ischus*—"His mighty power [*ischus*]." It refers to endowed power.

   Paul was saying that God has given believers unbelievable power. Many Christians claim they don't have enough strength or power. That's why Paul prayed for the believer to know the power available to him.

   (2) Demonstrated

       (*a*) Power to evangelize

           i) Romans 1:16—"I am not ashamed of the gospel of Christ; for it is the power of God unto salvation."

110

ii) 1 Thessalonians 1:5—"Our gospel came not unto you in word only, but also in power, and in the Holy Spirit, and in much assurance."

(b) Power to endure suffering

In 2 Corinthians 4:7 Paul says, "We have this treasure in earthen vessels, that the excellency of the power may be of God, and not of us." In verses 8-10 Paul details all the troubles and persecutions he had to endure for Christ's sake. Then in verse 14 he says, "Knowing that he who raised up the Lord Jesus shall raise us up also by Jesus."

(c) Power to do God's will

People often fear they don't have the energy or resources to do God's will. But Philippians 2:13 says, "It is God who worketh in you both to will and to do of his good pleasure."

(d) Power to serve

In Colossians 1:29 Paul says, "For this purpose also I labor, striving according to His power, which mightily works within me" (NASB).

(3) Delivered

(a) Acts 1:8—Jesus said, "Ye shall receive power, after the Holy Spirit is come upon you." The Holy Spirit came upon you when you were saved. So you do have the power.

(b) Ephesians 3:20—Paul said, "Now unto him who is able to do exceedingly abundantly above all that we ask or think, according to the power that worketh in us."

God has given us incredible power. Don't run around looking for something more. That's an affront to the gracious love of God who has given us everything in Christ.

b) His power illustrated (v. 20)

"Which he wrought in Christ, when he raised him from the dead, and set him at his own right hand in the heavenly places."

We may question God's power in our lives, but Paul tells us that it's the same power that raised Jesus from the dead and exalted Him to heaven. If you still aren't sure God will follow through on His promises, remember that He did so for Christ. We need to understand that God has the power to secure us and to fulfill the hope that is ours in Christ.

We all have a tendency to doubt if God will accomplish His plan. When we do we just need to remember that He fulfilled His plan for Christ. He raised Him out of the grave, shattered the chains of death, and drew Him to His side in heaven. He will do the same for us. There is no reason for us to be insecure.

3. The greatness of God's Person (vv. 21-23)

"Far above all principality, and power, and might, and dominion, and every name that is named, not only in this age, but also in that which is to come; and hath put all things under his feet, and gave him to be the head over all things to the church, which is his body, the fullness of him that filleth all in all."

a) Christ's ministry

It is vital we know that Christ is in us. He secures us, empowers us, and fulfills God's promises in us. We don't have anything to fear or lose. There is nothing more to seek because Christ is everything.

(1) To Timothy

Apparently Timothy was having some difficulties in his ministry. He may have been timid (2 Tim.

1:7-8) and discouraged because some of the people in his congregation were questioning his youth (1 Tim. 4:12). Some of the Ephesian errorists were confusing the believers with endless genealogies and myths (1 Tim. 1:3-4). Paul told Timothy to stir up the gift of God that was in him (2 Tim. 1:6) and organize his gifts (1 Tim. 4:14). But above all he needed to "Remember Jesus Christ, risen from the dead, descendant of David" (2 Tim. 2:8, NASB). Paul wanted Timothy to remember the greatness of the Person who lived within him. The phrase "descendant of David" refers to Christ's humanness—He understands us; He is sympathetic to our problems. The phrase "risen from the dead" refers to His deity—He is powerful enough to accomplish His good will through us. So remember who He is, and remember that He is in us.

(2) To believers

Every Christian ought to focus more on the person and power of Christ. Paul said, "We all, with unveiled face beholding as in a mirror the glory of the Lord, are changed into the same image from glory to glory, even as by the Spirit of the Lord" (2 Cor. 3:18). If we focus less on our problems and more on the person and power of Jesus Christ, we would be free from many of the problems we face.

b) Christ's rank

In Ephesians 1:21-22 Paul tells us that Christ is "far above all principality, and power, and might, and dominion." Those are all titles and ranks of angels. Christ is far above them all (Heb. 1:4-14). He also is far above "every name that is named, not only in this age, but also that which is to come, and hath put all things under his feet, and gave him to be the head over all things to the church, which is his body, the fullness of him that filleth all in all" (vv. 21-23). He is head over everything, including the church. Philippians 2:9-10 says His name "is above every name, that at the name of Jesus every knee should bow, of things in heaven, and things in earth, and things under the earth." We are filled with His fullness, and He has chosen to radiate Himself to the world through you. What a privilege.

Conclusion

God has a great plan for every believer. He brings it about with His great power and dwells within us to bring it to fulfillment. No wonder Paul said, "We are more than conquerors [Gk., *hupernikē*, "super conquerors"]" (Rom. 8:37). He also said, "We wrestle not against flesh and blood, but against principalities, against powers, against the rulers of the darkness of this world, against spiritual wickedness in high places" (Eph. 6:12). To combat those forces we need to "be strong in the Lord, and in the power of his might; put on the whole armor of God" (vv. 10-11). God's power is available to us.

The sixteenth-century French reformer John Calvin said regarding Ephesians 1:22-23, "This is the highest honour of the Church, that, until He is united to us, the Son of God reckons Himself in some measure imperfect. What consolation it is for us to learn, that, not until we are in His presence, does He possess all His parts, or does He wish to be regarded as complete!" (*Commentaries on the Epistles of Paul to the Galatians and Ephesians* [Grand Rapids: Baker, 1979], p. 218). The incomparable Christ is incomplete until the church, which is His body, is complete. Paul prayed that we might understand these great truths—and that is my prayer for you.

Focusing on the Facts

1. What is the "something more" that many people in Christianity are searching for today (see pp. 100-101)?
2. What does the search for something more do to the doctrine of salvation (see p. 101)?
3. Describe the problem that the Colossian church faced (Col. 2:8-23; see pp. 101-3).
4. How does Ephesians 1:3 apply to the search for something more (see p. 104)?
5. In American culture, what does the heart usually represent? What was the Jewish perspective (see p. 106)?

6. How did the Jewish people refer to emotions or feelings? Why (see p. 107)?
7. What does the heart usually refer to in Scripture (see p. 107)?
8. Does God appeal to our emotions or our mind? Why (see p. 107)?
9. Describe the problem Paul addresses in 2 Corinthians 6:11-13. What principle does that passage teach (see p. 108)?
10. What does it mean to be enlightened by divine truth? How does that occur (see p. 108)?
11. Why did Paul want his readers to understand their place in God's plan (see p. 109)?
12. What are the four Greek words used for power in Ephesians 1:19? What does each one mean (see p. 110)?
13. Why was Paul so concerned that believers understand the power given to them by God (see p. 110)?
14. What are four examples of the practical outworking of God's power in our lives (see pp. 110-11)?
15. What assurances from Scripture do we have that show we possess the power of God (see p. 111)?
16. How did Paul illustrate the effectiveness of God's power (see p. 112)?
17. What was Paul's main encouragement to Timothy (2 Tim. 2:8; see pp. 112-13)?
18. Why is it important for us to focus on the person and power of Christ (2 Cor. 3:18; see p. 113)?

Pondering the Principles

1. Are you seeking for something more? Are you seeking for something similar to the errors the Colossians were struggling with (see pp. 101-3)? Be honest in your evaluation. As a Christian, is there anything more to seek that isn't provided in salvation? Memorize 2 Peter 1:3 as a reminder.

2. Think of the last time you responded emotionally rather than rationally. Are you prone to respond to your emotions or your mind? What should you respond to? Why? How can you be sure that your responses are based on truth and not on feelings? Make more of an effort to read Scripture and memorize important passages. As you saturate your mind with Scripture, you will find your responses are based more on God's truth rather than your emotions.

3. Have you ever felt inadequate to evangelize, inadequate to endure persecution and suffering, and inadequate to live the Christian life? Review the section on the demonstration of God's power (see pp. 110-11). Then meditate on Ephesians 3:20 and commit it to memory.

8
Coming Alive in Christ

Outline

Introduction

Lesson
I. Salvation Is from Sin (vv. 1-3)
  A. The Alienation of Man (v. 1a)
    1. Physical death
    2. Spiritual death
  B. The Activity of Man (v. 1b)
    1. Sin described
      a) *Hamartia*
      b) *Paraptōma*
    2. Sin defined
      a) Missing God's standard
      b) Measuring man's failure
        (1) The recognition of human good
          (a) Luke 6:33
          (b) Luke 11:13
          (c) Acts 28:2
        (2) The conviction by the Holy Spirit
  C. The Atmosphere of Man (v. 2)
    1. The course of the world (v. 2a)
      a) Defined
      b) Demonstrated
        (1) Humanism
        (2) Materialism
        (3) Sex
    2. The prince of the power of the air (v. 2b)
      a) His identity
      b) His influence
  D. The Attributes of Man (v. 3)

Introduction

The book of Ephesians discusses the ramifications of a believer's being in Christ. In Ephesians 1:3-14 the apostle Paul presents God's master plan from eternity past. In verses 15-23 he prays that believers would understand that plan and all that it means to be in Christ. In chapter 2, however, he moves from eternity past into the present. He describes the process of salvation—the miracle that brought us into God's eternal plan.

Understanding God's Power

The apostle Paul wanted believers to understand "the exceeding greatness of his power toward us who believe, according to the working of his mighty power." To help us understand how tremendous that power is, he illustrates it in verse 20: It is the same power that "raised [Christ] from the dead, and set him at [God's] right hand." That's Paul's first illustration of God's power in Ephesians, and we already discussed it in detail (see p. 112). But in chapter 2 Paul gives a second illustration: that power raised you from the dead and exalted you to sit you at the right hand of God with Christ (vv. 5-6). So to understand God's power we must first look at the resurrection and exaltation of Christ, and then at our own resurrection and exaltation.

The natural response to that last thought is: "What do you mean I have been raised from the dead and exalted? When did that happen?" It happened spiritually, and it will occur physically in the future when your body is redeemed, resurrected, and exalted (Rom. 8:23). But God already has accomplished the resurrection and exaltation of your inner man. That's the miracle Paul discusses in chapter 2. In so doing he presents a great picture of the doctrine of salvation.

Lesson

As we examine Ephesians 2:1-10 we will see that Paul presents the believer's salvation in terms of his past (vv. 1-3), present (vv. 4-6), and future (vv. 7-10). But within that general context I want you to see six aspects of salvation.

I. SALVATION IS FROM SIN (vv. 1-3)

"You . . . who were dead in trespasses and sins; in which in times past ye walked according to the course of this world, according to the prince of the power of the air, the spirit that now worketh in the sons of disobedience; among whom also we all had our manner of life in times past in the lusts of our flesh, fulfilling the desires of the flesh and of the mind, and were by nature the children of wrath, even as others."

There is probably no clearer statement on the sinfulness of man in the New Testament than those three verses. Paul's first point is that we were sinners, which meant that we were spiritually dead.

A. The Alienation of Man (v. 1a)

"You . . . who were dead."

That phrase describes the condition of every person. We all were dead. If you are a Christian, death was your past reality. If you are not a Christian, death is your present condition—you're dead. Ephesians 4:18 explains what that means: It's to be "alienated from the life of God." It doesn't refer to physical deadness but to spiritual deadness. An unbeliever is dead to God.

119

1. Physical death

Physical death is best defined as an inability to respond to stimulus. A dead person can't react to anything. For example, some years ago while I was in my office, a boy banged on my door. Through his tears he pleaded with me to come with him. I followed him as he ran down the street to his house. When I arrived, his mother met me at the door. With tears streaming down her face, she pointed to a bedroom and said, "My baby is dead." I walked into the room and lying on the bed was a baby about three months old. I asked her if she tried to revive the baby and she said she had. Then she picked up the limp body, caressed the baby, kissed it, and cried, but the baby did not respond. An ambulance soon arrived, but the attendants were unable to revive the infant.

In terms of human relationships perhaps the strongest stimulus possible is the love of a mother for her baby. When that mother couldn't get a response out of her child, that was a prime example of physical death—the inability to respond.

2. Spiritual death

Likewise, spiritual death is an inability to respond to stimulus. God's love draws no response because a spiritually dead person is alienated from the life of God. He has no capacity to respond to God. But unlike a physically dead person, he is animate. The nineteenth-century Scottish commentator John Eadie described it as a case of "death walking" (*Commentary on the Epistle to the Ephesians* [Minneapolis: James and Klock, 1977], p. 121). Spiritually dead people are like zombies—they don't know they're dead and they're still going through the motions of living.

Jesus combined the concepts of physical and spiritual death in Matthew 8. He called a certain man to follow Him and be His disciple, but the man said, "Lord, permit me first to go and bury my father" (v. 21). But Jesus said, "Follow me, and let the dead bury their dead." Jesus was saying, "Let the spiritually dead bury the physically dead." The implication was that He had better plans for the man. In 1 Timothy 5:6 Paul refers to the widow who lives for pleasure as being "dead while she liveth."

B. The Activity of Man (v. 1b)

"In trespasses and sins."

Man is not dead because he commits sin but because he was born sinful. Think of it this way: A man is not a liar because he lies; he lies because he is a liar by nature. Jesus said, "That which cometh out of the man, that defileth the man" (Mark 7:20). Man is dead and lives in a state of sinfulness. The Greek word translated "in" is called a locative of sphere, which refers to the sphere in which we live. Thus Paul is saying that man is dead because he lives in the realm of sin.

1. Sin described

a) *Hamartia*—This Greek word, translated "sins" in Ephesians 2:1, is a hunter's word that means "to miss the target" or "to miss the mark."

b) *Paraptōma*—This Greek word, translated "trespasses" in verse 1, means "to slip," "to fall," or "to go the wrong direction."

Commentators through the years have tried to make distinctions between those two words, but I believe they are two ways of looking at the same thing.

2. Sin defined

a) Missing God's standard

Sin is a failure to hit God's target. Romans 3:23 says, "All have sinned, and come short of the glory of God." Sin is a failure to glorify God. Romans 1:21 says, "When they knew God, they glorified him not as God."

When the Bible says that every person is a sinner, it doesn't mean that everyone is at the same level of sinfulness. Twenty dead corpses lying side by side could all be at various degrees of decay. So it is with man: All are dead, but there are variances in decadence. Ultimately sin is not an issue of decay but a question of falling short of righteousness.

We understand that robbers, murderers, rapists, and liars are sinners. But sin is not so much an issue of what you do but of what you fail to do. And man is a sinner because he fails to glorify God. In Matthew 5:48 Jesus says, "Be ye, therefore, perfect, even as your Father, who is in heaven, is perfect." Man fails at that point, too. First Peter 1:16 says we are to be that way "because it is written, Be ye holy; for I am holy" (Lev. 11:44). Man falls short of glory, holiness, and perfection. There may be different levels of morality and different degrees of decadence, but every person falls short.

How Far Can You Jump?

Suppose we had a contest to see who could jump to Catalina Island from the beach at Los Angeles. You even could have as long a run as you wanted. When we jumped each of us would land at different spots in the water, but none of us would reach Catalina. The same thing is true spiritually. There are different levels of human attainment and different standards of morality, but no one can reach God's glory, perfection, and holiness. That can be attained only through Jesus Christ, whose righteousness is imputed to us when we are saved.

b) Measuring man's failure

Men and women try to jump to perfection, but they land in the sea of sin. Behavioral sins are the result of man's failure to reach God's standard.

(1) The recognition of human good

There are many people in this world we might say are good. You might know a non-Christian who is a great humanitarian and a wonderful

122

husband and father. There certainly isn't anything wrong with that.

(*a*) Luke 6:33—Jesus said, "If ye do good to them who do good to you, what thanks have ye? For sinners do the same." Indeed, sinners do good, but Jesus still identified them as sinners. In God's eyes sin isn't an issue of what people do for others. You can't claim to be righteous just because you do good to others. Doing good to others doesn't help a person live a holy and perfect life, which is God's standard.

(*b*) Luke 11:13—Jesus said, "If ye then, being evil, know how to give good gifts unto your children, how much more shall your heavenly Father give the Holy Spirit to them that ask him?" People give good gifts to their children, yet the Lord characterizes them as evil. Their evil is not manifested in what they do—giving good gifts to their children—but in what they don't do and can't do—bringing glory and honor to God.

(*c*) Acts 28:2—Paul and company had been shipwrecked on the island of Malta. Luke said that the natives showed them "extraordinary kindness" (NASB). Ungodly pagans showed great kindness to Paul, but good works are not enough to please God.

(2) The conviction by the Holy Spirit

In John 16:8 Jesus says to His disciples, "When he [the Holy Spirit] is come, he will reprove the world of sin." The Holy Spirit would come and convict people of sin. Verse 9 specifies what sin: "Because they believe not on me." Men don't live to the glory of God, and they are not perfect or holy. Why? Because they don't believe in Jesus Christ. No matter what else they might do, they're floundering in the ocean a long way from

123

the goal. You can't please God if you don't believe in Jesus Christ (John 5:22-23).

Man is dead—dead because of his inability to reach God's standard. He is a death-walking zombie manifesting a total inability to accomplish God's standard, even though he manifests moral goodness from time to time.

C. The Atmosphere of Man (v. 2)

1. The course of the world (v. 2a)

"In which in times past ye walked according to the course of this world [Gk., *kosmos*, "age"]."

Man is a victim of the spirit of the age, but he frequently claims to be doing exactly what he wants to do. One of my football coaches claimed to be a Christian but said he was going to do whatever he wanted. In reality he wasn't doing what he wanted but what the world dictated. He was walking according to the course of this age.

a) Defined

Kosmos doesn't refer to the physical world but to the ideological world of sin—the evil world system. The spiritual zombie indulges in the sins of the times. He lives according to the world's current standards. He is in complete harmony with the ~~zeitgeist~~—the spirit of the age.

Satan, the prince of this world (John 12:31), dominates the *kosmos* and pressures man to succumb to what the system tells him to do. That is total depravity—people walking in sin according to the spirit of the age. They are walking in a circle they can't escape from on their own.

b) Demonstrated

What is the spirit of the age? I believe three things best characterize our age.

124

(1) Humanism—The philosophy of humanism suggests that you do as you please—sometimes at the expense of others.

(2) Materialism—The philosophy of materialism says that we live to obtain more money and possessions. Many Christians find this philosophy difficult to resist.

(3) Sex—Everything from *a* to *z* is promoted with sex. You practically have to drive with your eyes closed to avoid billboards that contain overt sexual overtones!

One writer said that we don't have even the morals of a barnyard. Humanism, materialism, and sex are the spirit of our age.

2. The prince of the power of the air (v. 2*b*)

"According to the prince of the power of the air, the spirit that now worketh in the sons of disobedience."

a) His identity

The prince (Gk., *archos*) is none other than Satan. The world has its *archos*, but we have the *kephalē* ("head")—Jesus Christ. Satan, the leader of the demons, rules over the world system. That doesn't mean he indwells everyone as he indwelt Judas (John 13:29). But it does mean he is behind the influences and trends in the world. His demons carry out his objectives, whether they are secular or religious.

b) His influence

The Greek word translated "air" in verse 2 could refer to the atmosphere around the earth—the first heaven. (The second heaven is the stellar atmosphere, and the third heaven is God's domain.) Some scholars believe that Satan exists around the earth in the first heaven, fighting holy angels and leading his demons. Occasionally he may even enter the third heaven to accuse us before the throne of God as he did Job (Job 1:6-12; 2:1-7).

But "air" can also refer to the realm of ideas. We often say there's a certain "air in the room" when we want to refer to an attitude. Just as "world" refers to an ideology, "air" is most likely the same. Satan functions not only in the physical atmosphere but also in the ideological realm. He promotes his concepts and breeds his ideas. He is behind the whole system, which is straight from hell.

Satan is "the spirit that now worketh in the sons of disobedience" (Eph. 2:2). He draws man into active disobedience against God.

D. The Attributes of Man (v. 3)

"Among whom also we all had our manner of life in times past in the lusts of our flesh, fulfilling the desires of the flesh and of the mind, and were by nature the children of wrath, even as others."

The death walker meanders through a system controlled by Satan. He functions only in response to his flesh. The Greek word translated "lusts" (*epithumia*) refers to strong, evil passions. The Greek word translated "desires" (*thelēma*) means "drives." So the passion turns into a drive. Men are driven to fulfill "the desires of the flesh [his fallen nature] and of the mind." So man is physically and mentally driven into active sin and trespasses. He follows the pattern of disobedience when his lusts develop into drives that compel him to fulfill what his body and mind demand. By nature he is a child of wrath. As such he is the target of God's judgment. That concludes a vivid description of man's total depravity.

II. SALVATION IS BY LOVE (v. 4)

"But God, who is rich in mercy, for his great love with which he loved us."

126

It is God who rescues man from a state of living death. He is rich (Gk., *plousiōs*, "overabounding") with mercy for the sinner. If we got what we deserved we'd be in trouble. But God is merciful, holding back what we deserve.

God is merciful because of His "great love with which he loved us." Salvation is based on love. God doesn't save people based on their worthiness; He chooses them based on His love. His intrinsic, essential attribute of love manifests itself to us in His grace and mercy. Love is His motive. He reaches out to vile, sinful, godless, ungrateful, unworthy, unholy, destitute, depraved human beings engulfed in sins and trespasses in the service of Satan.

A Sin Against Love

Man's sin is not so much a crime against God's law as it is a sin against His love. Suppose someone was driving too fast on a neighborhood street and killed a child playing in the street. He would be charged with manslaughter and speeding. Then he would be tried and likely be found guilty. If so, he would either have to pay a fine or be imprisoned. After paying his fine or serving his sentence, the law would be satisfied. But that's true only regarding his sin against the law.

What about the child's mother? Could he ever make up for the loss of her child by paying a fine or serving a sentence? No. From her perspective he sinned against her love, not against the law. The only way he could ever be restored to her would be if she offered him free and unconditional forgiveness. And that is precisely what God has done. Man has not only sinned against God's law but killed His Son as well. And he continues to do so by his constant rejection and open defiance of Him. Yet God reaches out and offers unconditional and complete forgiveness to those who accept it.

III. SALVATION RESULTS IN LIFE (v. 5)

"Even when we were dead in sins, [He] hath made us alive together with Christ (by grace ye are saved)."

The one thing a dead man needs most is life. And that's what God provides. If you ever doubt the power of God in your life, remember it is the same power that raised Christ from the dead and you from your sin. If you're not sure God can get you into heaven or that He can get you out of the grave at the resurrection, just remember that He already raised you spiritually. The physical resurrection is the easier task. We can have confidence in God's power.

When you became a Christian, you ceased being alienated from the life of God—you became alive. You became sensitive to God. You could understand the Bible because the Holy Spirit was in your life teaching you. You had a reason to live. You felt God at work in your life. You knew Christ. There was an immediate brotherhood with other Christians. You became the possessor of eternal life.

When God raised Christ from the grave, He made us alive together with Him. In a sense we were with Him when He rose from the dead, and that means God's power has already been displayed on our behalf.

IV. SALVATION IS WITH A PURPOSE (vv. 6-7)

A. To Seat Us in the Heavenlies (v. 6)

"[God] hath raised us up together, and made us sit together in the heavenly places in Christ Jesus."

1. The fact of our exaltation

When God raised us from the dead He didn't leave us in the cemetery. After Jesus raised Lazarus from the dead, he was still wrapped in his grave clothes, so Jesus said, "Loose him, and let him go" (John 11:44). Christ first performed the miracle of resurrection for us, then He did a second miracle: He exalted us to a seat in the heavenly places. And that is a past-tense reality—we already are seated there positionally.

Philippians 3:20 says that our "citizenship is in heaven." Because we are saved we are no longer of this world. We have eternal life. We are alive to God; we merely live in this dead world. But our life is in heaven, "hidden with Christ in God" (Col. 3:3). That's why Ephesians 1:3 says He "hath blessed us with all spiritual blessings in heavenly places in Christ."

2. The focus of our exaltation

To be in heavenly places obviously doesn't mean your physical body is now in heaven. Your mind, however, exists in God's domain. All your blessings are there. The Father, Christ, and the Holy Spirit are there. All believers who died are there. Heaven is your home—it's your world.

B. To Shower Us with Kindness (v. 7)

"That in the ages to come he might show the exceeding riches of his grace in his kindness toward us through Christ Jesus."

God saved you so He could be kind to you forever. But why would He be kind to people who don't deserve it? Because God is love (1 John 4:8), and love is kind (1 Cor. 13:4). God saved us not only to keep us out of hell but also to shower us with the riches of His grace.

From the moment of salvation, and continuing throughout eternity, we are the recipients of "the exceeding riches of his grace." God doesn't withhold anything—He gives us everything through Jesus Christ. After pouring out His grace on us, God shows us off to the angels so that they can praise Him for His grace and give Him glory. God's glory is at stake, and He will never allow that to be diminished. If He receives glory by pouring out His grace on you, He will do it (and has done it).

V. SALVATION IS THROUGH FAITH (vv. 8-9)

"By grace are ye saved through faith; and that not of yourselves, it is the gift of God—not of works, lest any man should boast."

If we were responsible for our own salvation we would receive the glory for it. But Christ did all the work to accomplish salvation by dying on the cross. Just before He died He said, "It is finished" (John 19:30). So the glory all belongs to God.

A. Faith Illustrated

We're all creatures of faith. We live by faith every day. Every time you drink a can of soda, it's an act of faith. You don't have any idea what's really in that can. Whenever you eat in a restaurant you can't be sure of what they are serving you. You have to exhibit faith every time you turn on your faucet and drink water.

The faith that is basic to human nature is what God uses to draw you to Himself. If you can have faith in the things I just described, you ought to be able to trust the God of the universe. The essence of faith is believing and accepting His gift of salvation.

B. Faith Induced

The moment you accept God's gift is the moment you come alive spiritually. If you are a Christian, God released His power in your life to accomplish the work of salvation. You don't ever need to question God's power—you've already seen it at work. According to verses 1-3 you were dead. But now you are saved through faith. You didn't do it; it was God's gift to you. If works on your part were involved, you would boast; but the privilege of boasting about your salvation belongs to God.

You can breathe spiritually because God slapped you on the backside to make you breathe. You can hear with the ear of faith because God unplugged your ears. Salvation is not the result of your confirmation, baptism, communion, church attendance or membership, giving to the church or to charity, keeping the Ten Commandments, living by the Sermon on the Mount, believing in God, being a good neighbor, or living a respectable life. None of those things will ever allow anyone into heaven. Hell will be full of people who do those things thinking that will save them.

VI. SALVATION PRODUCES GOOD WORKS (v. 10)

"We are his workmanship, created in Christ Jesus unto good works, which God hath before ordained that we should walk in them."

A. The Manifestation of Good Works

The result of salvation is good works. In John 15:8 Jesus says, "In this is my Father glorified, that ye bear much fruit." When God saves you He wants to see good works produced in your life because that manifests His power. His power saved you, and when your good works reveal that, He receives glory.

B. The Meaning of Good Works

The Bible refers to many different kinds of works. There are the works of the law (Gal. 2:16; 3:11), the works of the flesh (Gal. 5:19-21), the works of darkness (Rom. 13:12; Eph. 5:11), and dead works (Heb. 6:1). However, none of those are the kind of works Ephesians 2:10 describes. Paul was referring to the works that are the result of salvation, not the works that men do in a futile effort to save themselves.

C. The Masterpiece of Good Works

The Greek word translated "workmanship" in Ephesians 2:10 came to mean "masterpiece." We are God's masterpiece. From the beginning His design was to conform us to Christ, our good works being the proof of our salvation. God's power is at work in your life, shaping you into the image of Jesus Christ. You are God's masterpiece!

Conclusion

Who is the true Christian? The one who does good works. Many people claim to be saved, but only those who do good as a result of

131

their salvation to the glory of God are truly saved. I hope you are one of them.

Focusing on the Facts

1. What are Paul's two illustrations of God's power in Ephesians 1-2 (see p. 118)?
2. According to Ephesians 2:1 and 4:18, what is the root of man's problem (see p. 119)?
3. Explain commentator John Eadie's term "death-walking" (see p. 120).
4. What two concepts did Jesus combine in Matthew 8:21 (see p. 120)?
5. Are people spiritually dead because they commit sin or because they they are born sinful? Explain (see p. 121).
6. Translate and define the Greek words *hamartia* and *paraptōma* (see p. 121).
7. What is the biblical definition of sin (see pp. 121-22)?
8. Man falls short of what (see p. 122)?
9. Since Jesus did not deny that people do good things, why are those same people referred to as "sinners" (see p. 123)?
10. The phrase "the course of this world" refers to what (Eph. 2:2; see p. 124)?
11. What three words characterize the spirit of our age (see pp. 124-25)?
12. Who is "the prince of the power of the air" (Eph. 2:2; see p. 125)?
13. The term *air* refers to what (see pp. 125-26)?
14. What is the difference between the "lusts" of the flesh and the "desires" of the flesh (Eph. 2:3; see p. 126)?
15. God's grace is His giving us what we don't deserve. Contrast that with His mercy (see pp. 126-27).
16. Illustrate the difference between a sin against the law and a sin against love. What is the only way that a sin against love can be reconciled (see p. 127)?
17. In what way have we been raised from the dead and seated in the heavenly places (Eph. 2:6; see pp. 128-29)?
18. Why did God save us (Eph. 2:7; see p. 129)?
19. Explain why we all can be described as creatures of faith (see p. 130).

20. Who is responsible for your salvation? Explain (see p. 130).
21. What is the importance of good works in the life of a Christian (Eph. 2:10; see p. 131)?

Pondering the Principles

1. Read Ephesians 2:1-3. As you do, substitute personal pronouns in the appropriate places. How does that make you want to respond to God? With those verses in mind, are we to view the unsaved as our enemies or as prisoners of the enemy? Why? How can having a proper perspective of the unsaved change our attitudes toward them? Do you have an unsaved acquaintance whom you've been treating as an enemy? Ask the Lord to help you see him or her as someone for whom He died.

2. Read Colossians 3 and note the characteristics of the old man and the new man. Write down some personal characteristics of sin in your life before you were saved. Next to those characteristics, record the specific changes that have taken place since you became a Christian. Thank God for His transforming power.

3. The majority of unbelievers think they will go to heaven if they are good enough or if their good deeds outweigh their bad ones. How would you illustrate the error of that kind of thinking to them (see p. 122)? To prepare yourself to respond to the prevalent error of salvation by works, memorize one of the following passages: Galatians 2:16, Ephesians 2:8-10, 2 Timothy 1:9, or Titus 3:5.

4. According to Ephesians 2:10, why will good works be present in the life of a truly regenerated person? According to Matthew 5:16 and John 15:8, why do Christians do good works? How do our good works sometimes fall short of their intended purpose? Ask God to make you more aware of the times when your good works glorify you more than they glorify Him.

133

Scripture Index

137

Topical Index

Adoption, spiritual, 55-56
Apostleship, credentials identifying, 18-19
Asceticism, Christ plus, 103
Atonement. *See* Redemption

Blessings, spiritual. *See* Resources in Christ
Body, the. *See* Church

Calvin, John, on Ephesians 1:22-23, 114
Charis. See Grace
Christian life. *See* Resources in Christ
Church, the
  Body of Christ, 10, 15-16, 22, 24-25, 38-39
  eternal formation of. *See* Election
  function of, 39, 49
  metaphors of, 15-16
  mystery of, 10, 13-16
  purpose of, 38-39
  unity of. *See* Body of Christ
Citizenship, heavenly, 30-31, 128-29
Colossians
  problems of the, 102-3
  purpose of the epistle of, 101-2

Death
  physical, 120
  spiritual, 119-26
Depravity, total. *See* Sin

Eadie, John, on spiritual death, 120

Election
  of the church, 26, 32-35, 39-48, 73, 109
  foreknowledge and, 44-45
  importance of, 41-42
  irresistible nature of, 43-44, 74
  motive behind, 46-47
  objects of, 33-34, 43, 45
  paradox of, 32, 36, 40-41, 75-76
  purpose of, 33-34, 46-47, 73-75, 80-81
  response to, 76
  results of, 47
  theocratic, 33, 42
  time of, 45
  vocational, 42-43
Emotions, obstruction by, 107-8, 115
Enlightenment. *See* Holy Spirit
Ephesians
  audience of the book of, 17-18
  faith of the, 89-91
  love of the, 91-92
Exhortation, improper, 86

Faith
  genuine, 89-92
  illustrations of, 130
  love and, 92
  salvation and. *See* Salvation
Feelings. *See* Emotions
Foreknowledge. *See* Election
Forgiveness
  contrasted, 56
  definition of, 55
  extent of, 60-61, 63
  gift of, 60-63

God
glory of. *See* Election
goodness of, 36
kindness of. *See* love of
love of, 126-27, 129
power of, 110-12, 118-19
promises of. *See* Promises of
God
trustworthiness of. *See* Promises of God
Grace, as a greeting, 20
Green, Hetty, greed of, 8
Guilt
attempts to alleviate, 61
fact of, 61-62
manipulation by, 86
reason for, 62
value of, 61

Hearst, William Randolph,
needless search of, 93
Heart, meaning of, 106-9
Holy Spirit, the
enlightenment by. *See* illumination by
illumination by, 94-95, 105-9.
See also Resources in
Christ
receiving, 94, 105
seal of, 77-80
wisdom of. *See* illumination
by
Humanism, philosophy of, 125

Illumination. *See* Holy Spirit
Inheritance in Christ. *See* Resources in Christ
"The Inner Life," 44
Intellect, importance of the,
106-7

Jesus Christ
blood of, 58-59
Body of. *See* Church

focusing on, 113
knowing, 95
lordship of, 90-91
rank of, 113-14
resources in. *See* Resources in
Christ
sufficiency of, 100-15
union with. *See* Resources in
Christ
Justification
contrasted, 56
description of, 55

Kingdom, the
millennial. *See* Millennial
kingdom
mystery, 11-14

Legalism, Christ plus, 102-3
Life, meaning of, 64, 68
Love
faith and, 92
genuine, 91-92, 97
"in the Lord," 91, 97
sin against, 127

MacArthur, John, encounter
with dead baby, 120
Macbeth, despair of, 64
Man, fallen nature of. *See* Sin
Manipulation. *See* Guilt
Materialism, philosophy of, 125
Maturity. *See* Resources in
Christ
Maurois, André, relativism of,
63-64
Millennial kingdom, the
anticipation of, 12
literal nature of, 13-14
offering of, 12
postponement of, 12-13
rejection of, 12
Monasticism. *See* Asceticism

Moody Press, a ministry of the Moody Bible Institute, is designed for edu-
cation, evangelization, and edification. If we may assist you in knowing
more about Christ and the Christian life, please write us without obliga-
tion: Moody Press, c/o MLM, Chicago, Illinois 60610.